Discover God

Discover God through His Attributes

Rita Kroon

A Walk to the Well

Dedicated to:

All who desire to know God intimately,
and respond to His invitation to do so through prayer;
to my daughters and their husbands,
my grandchildren, and my sister,
to all my loved ones who give special meaning
to the name family,
and to the Lord God Almighty
Who has revealed Himself to man for His own glory
and for our joy and to delight in Him.

Special Dedication to:

*My current works are in loving memory of
my husband, Burt, and
our daughter, René,
each with whom I shared such
an intimacy with Jesus.*

Rita Kroon

ACKNOWLEDGEMENTS

Mere words could never express my deep love & appreciation to Burt, my husband, who has given me the freedom to spend endless hours researching, reading, and writing. He is supportive, attentive, and encourages me throughout the long process of writing a book. Thanks, Swedie, I love you forever.

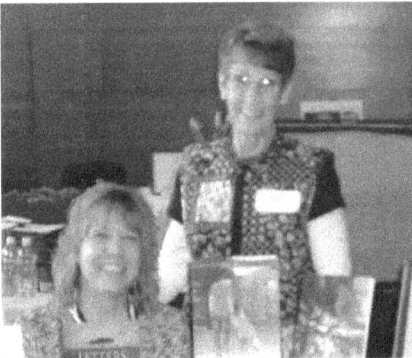

I am beyond grateful to my daughter, LaDawn for the unselfish time she spent at my computer making certain details were accurate and concise. Without her help and dedication, I would not have been able to complete this book. Thanks, Sunshine. Love you.

"He who consciously or unconsciously has chosen to ignore God is an orphan in the universe."

Emile Calliet, in *Alone a High Noon*

Introduction

ATTRIBUTES: Qualities, characteristics, and features which describe God and are separate from the limited or relative attributes of man.

Some attributes are exclusive to God and are called *divine* (cannot be imparted to another) such as **infinity** (without beginning and without end); also referred to as *absolute* (perfect) such as **omniscient** (to have perfect knowledge of everything that is past, present, or future at the same time), as well as *immanent* (indwelt) such as **transcendent** (God is above His creation, and He would exist even if there were no creation. His existence is apart from all His creation of heaven and earth, seen and unseen

Attributes found in man, such as **love,** are considered *communicable* (transferable); *relative* (imperfect and pertaining to man); and *transitive* (conveyed to another).

God's attributes in relationship to His creation may also be called *communicable.* An example of this would be righteousness - Jesus transferred His righteous to those who have put their faith and trust in Him as Lord and Savior.

God is **indivisible**. God exists in three persons, Father, Son, and Holy Spirit. Each of the three is distinguished from the other; each possesses all the divine attributes, yet the three are one. God is one God. *Hear, O Israel! The Lord is our God, the Lord is one!* (Deuteronomy 6:4) The indivisibility has to do with God's essence; the Trinity has to do with God's being. "Go, therefore and make disciples of all the nations, baptizing them in the name of the *Father* and the *Son* and the *Holy Spirit*." (Matthew 28:19) Thus, **indivisible** is an attribute of God that is absolute or pertains to God alone.

Because God is God—He is beyond man's comprehension. His ways, His character, and His thoughts are higher than man's thoughts or understanding. If man could understand all who God is, such as having no beginning or end and being three persons in one God (Father, Son, and Holy Spirit), God would not be worthy of man's worship.

God loves His creation, and because He especially loves man, who was created in His image, He chose to reveal Himself to mankind through His written word - the Scriptures/the Bible and through His Holy Spirit so that He would be our God and we would be His people.

Man was created to worship God and to know the joy that comes from being in an intimate relationship with the Creator of the entire universe.

Come! Discover who God is through His Attributes.

Rita Kroon

Contents

$\mathcal{A}$

Discover God as

Accessible – *God is easy to approach by those with a humble heart, and indeed, He invites all to come near to Him.*

Lord God, from the beginning when You made Adam and Eve, you were accessible to them. You have said that if I seek You, I will find You when I search for You with all my heart. You drew even nearer to people 2000 years ago when You sent Your beloved and only begotten Son Jesus Christ who dwelt among humanity displaying Your glory. You gave Your Holy Spirit to indwell those who believe in You making Yourself accessible in the most intimate way possible. You invite all who are weary and heavy laden to come to You and You will give rest. Thank You that You are not a god far off, but One who draws near. You are my God, and I am Your child. Thank you for assuring me that when I pray, You hear my prayers and will answer them. **Jeremiah 29:13; John 14:6; John 15:26**

All-Knowing - *God knows all actual and potential things - past, present, and future.*

Lord of the heavens and the earth, could anyone teach You knowledge? You are the One who judges those on high! Yes, even the angels. You are all-knowing. You know the number of stars and their names for You made them and set them in their places in the universe, and not one is missing. You know me. You have called me by name. I am in awe because there is no one like You. I praise Your holy name! **Job 21:22;   Psalms 147:4**

Lord God, I worship You for You teach man knowledge, and You know the thoughts of man - discerning man's thoughts from afar. You search all hearts, and you know the intent of all man's thoughts. The mind of man plans his way, but You, O Lord, direct his steps. You know what is before and behind and there is nothing hidden from You. You know the end from the beginning and from ancient times things that are not yet done. Therefore, I praise You for You alone are all-knowing and worthy to be praised. **Psalm 94:11;   Proverbs 16:9;   Isaiah 46:10**

Who has directed You, O Spirit of the Lord, or what counselor has informed You? With whom would You consult or who could give You understanding? Who could teach You the path of justice or knowledge? What man has informed You of the way of understanding? There is no one, Lord, for You are all-knowing and the source of all wisdom, and I worship You. **Isaiah 40:13-14**

Almighty – *is a translation of the divine title of Shaddai and always emphasizes God's complete power over everything in the universe.*

Almighty God, there is safety in abiding under Your shadow. I will not fear the terrors of the night nor the destruction that happens at noonday, but I will trust in You for You will give Your angels charge over me to keep me in all my ways. I believe the angel who declared that You are He who is and who was and who is to come, the Almighty. Your judgments are righteous and true. Therefore, I delight in You, and may You bless me with more awareness of Your presence. **Psalm 91:1,11; Revelation 4:8, 16:7**

Who could search out the deep things of You, O God, or who could find the limits of You, the Almighty, for You do great things beyond man's comprehension and wonderous works without measure? Who is mighty like You? Who is called Great, the Mighty God, whose name is Lord of hosts? There is not one greater or mightier than You and so I bow before You in adoration and worship.
Job 9:10, 11:7-9; Psalm 89:8, 147:5;
Jeremiah 32:17

Alpha and Omega – *Alpha and Omega are the first and last letters of the Greek alphabet and mean the Almighty God from beginning to the end of all creation.*

Jesus said, "I am the Alpha and the Omega, the Beginning and the End, who is and who was and who is to come, the Almighty." Jesus said to John, "It is done! I am the Alpha and the Omega, the Beginning and the End." Again, Jesus said, "I am the Alpha and the Omega, the Beginning and the End, the First and the Last." I worship You, Lord Jesus, because Your Word is true. Blessed be those who put their trust in You.   **Revelation 1:8, 21:6, 22:13**

Lord of the heavens and the earth, You are the Alpha and the Omega who is and who was and who is to come, the Almighty. You are the beginning and the end of all things - seen and unseen. We praise You with the hosts of heaven who say, "Give praise to our God all who fear Him." Their voices, like mighty peals of thunder say, "Hallelujah! For the Lord our God, the Almighty, reigns."   **Revelation 19:5-6**

Awesome – *God's works of creation, redemption, sovereignty, judgment, and forgiveness are astounding. God is wondrous and perfect.*

Lord, there is no One like You among the gods; there is none like You who is majestic in holiness, awesome in praises, and in working wonders. You

4

alone are worthy to be worshiped, my Lord and my God. **Exodus 15:11**

I need not fear nor have any dread, for You, O Lord God, are in my midst. You are a great and awesome God, and there is no other. You are exalted in power and Your majesty fills the heavens and the earth. Come, all the earth, shout joyfully to God; sing the glory of His matchless name; make His praise glorious. Say with me, "How awesome are Your works. How awesome is Your power! Let us exalt His name together. Let us sing to the Lord as long as we live. Let us sing praise to our God while we have our being.
Deuteronomy 7:21; Job 37:22-23; Psalm 66:1-3, 104:33

Shout joyfully to our God all the earth; sing the glory of His name; make His praise glorious. Say to God, "How astounding are Your works!" Let us sing to the Lord as long as we live. Let us sing praise to our awesome God while we have our being.
Psalm 66:1-3, 104:33

I will extol You, my God and King, and I will praise Your name forever for You are an awesome God. You are great and highly to be praised. Every generation shall declare Your mighty acts. I will meditate on the glorious splendor of Your majesty and tell of Your greatness. Men shall speak of the power of Your mighty acts, my God, and my King. I will praise you all the days of my life and forevermore. **Psalm145:1-6**

Discover God and praise Him for He is Accessible, All-knowing, Almighty, Alpha and Omega, and Awesome.

*****

B

Discover God as

Beautiful – *God's beauty, together with his virtue, humbles the soul of humanity.*

The psalmist says, "One thing I have asked from the Lord—that I shall seek: that I may dwell in the house of the Lord all the days of my life, to gaze on the beauty of the Lord, and to meditate in His temple." I magnify You, O my Lord, for Your beauty is like no other's.   **Psalms 27:4-5**

The prophets proclaim, "A day is coming when the Branch of the Lord will be beautiful and glorious. All eyes will see the Messiah and bow at His feet and proclaim, "Beautiful is the King who shall rule and prosper and execute judgment and righteousness in the earth." Your beauty is only glimpsed, O Lord, in Your creation, and I still marvel and give You all the glory!   **Isaiah 4:2; Jeremiah 23:5, 33:15**

Beloved – *Jesus is the heavenly Father's only begotten, beloved Son and is divinely and deeply loved by the Father.*

O, to be at the Jordan River and behold the heavens opened and see the Spirit of God descending as a dove upon You, Lord Jesus. O, to hear a voice come out from heaven and say such beautiful words, "This is My Beloved Son, in whom I am well-pleased." Or, to be standing with Peter, James, and John on a high mountain and see You be transfigured before my very eyes. I can only imagine what awe I would have felt to see you enshrouded in a cloud, and hear a voice from heaven say, "This is My Beloved Son, listen to Him!" I would fall on my knees and worship You, O Most Beloved of Your Father. Even now, as I read the words of Scripture spoken by the God of the heavens, I marvel at Your greatness, Lord Jesus.
Matthew 3:17, 17:5

Heavenly Father, You fulfilled the words spoken by Isaiah when You said of Jesus, "Behold, My Servant whom I have chosen, My Beloved in whom My soul is well-pleased; I will put My Spirit upon Him, and He shall proclaim justice to the Gentiles. He will not quarrel, nor cry out, nor will anyone hear His voice in the streets. A battered reed He will not break off, and a smoldering wick He will not put out, until he leads justice to victory. And in His name the Gentiles will hope." Father, You exemplified Your Beloved Son's graciousness and gentleness. And so, I worship You, my Lord and my God.   **Matthew 12:18-21**

I praise the glory of Your grace which You freely bestowed on us in the Beloved.   **Ephesians 1:6**

I give thanks to You, heavenly Father, for You have qualified us to share in the inheritance of the saints in light, for You delivered us from the domain of darkness, and transferred us to the kingdom of Your Beloved Son in whom we have the forgiveness of sins.   **Colossians 1:12-13**

Boundless – *God is not confined by space nor limited by time. His presence has no boundaries.*

God of the heavens and the earth, will heaven and the heaven of heavens be able to contain You? Would a temple made by man be able to restrain You? Will you indeed, dwell with man on earth, to accommodate Yourself to the low position of humanity to fellowship with them? Because You are boundless in scope and limitless in time, I magnify Your name, O God, who is greater than all the space of the universe.   **2 Chronicles 2:6, 6:18**

The Lord said to Isaiah, "Heaven is My throne, and earth is My footstool. Where is the house that you will build Me? And where is the place of My rest? Has My hand not made all these things." I glorify Your name, O Lord, for are boundless and cannot be confined by anything You have made and certainly not temples made with hands. You are God and I worship You!   **Isaiah 66:1**

Bountiful - *God is generous, even extravagant, in giving gifts and favor.*

How precious are Your thoughts to me, O God! How vast is the sum of them! If I could count them, they would be more than the sand. I am reminded You are bountiful, and You lavish Your richest blessings on me. I praise You and I am eternally grateful. **Psalm 139:17-18**

Thank You, Father, for the invitation to ask, to seek, to knock, for You say that if Ask we will receive, and if we seek, we find and if we knock, it will be opened. And again, You say that if we, being evil, know how to give good gifts to our children, how much more will You give what is good to those who ask You. Thank you again, Father. **Matthew 7:7, 11**

O God, You are rich in mercy, because of the great love with which You loved us—even when we were dead in our transgressions—You made us alive in Christ Jesus and raised us up with Him in the heavenly places so that in the ages to come, You might show the bountiful riches of Your grace in kindness toward us in Christ Jesus. How I rejoice to know believers will be an eternal display of Your grace. Thank you, Father. **Ephesians 2:4-7**

Discover God and Worship Him because He is Beautiful, Beloved, Boundless, and Bountiful.

C

Discover God as

Comforter - _Refers to the Spirit of truth, the Holy Spirit gives us comfort, will teach us all things, will bring all things to remembrance, and indwells all believers._

Lord, if You had not been my help, surely my soul would soon have dwelt in the abode of darkness. Surely, I soon would have died. If I should say, "My foot has slipped," Your loving kindness, O Lord, will hold me up. When my anxious thoughts multiply within me, Your consolations, Your comfort, delights my soul. I give thanksgiving to You, O Comforter.
Psalm 94:17-19

Listen to the words of the Lord, O my soul, and be comforted for the Lord says, "I, even I, am He who comforts you. Who are you that you are afraid of man who dies, and of the son of man who is made like grass that you have forgotten the Lord your Maker, who stretched out the heavens and laid the foundations of the earth? I am the Lord your God, the Holy One of Israel, your Savior." My soul delights in You, O Lord, for You have comforted me in my distress. **Isaiah 51:12**

Blessed is the name of the Lord Almighty God for You comfort those who mourn. Blessed is the name of our Deliverer for You wipe away our tears and death shall be no more. We lift up our eyes to You, O mighty God, for You will cause all pain to cease, and our crying will be no more. Bless the Lord, O my soul, for He comforts me through His Holy Spirit.
Matthew 5:4; Revelation 21:4

Blessed be You, God, and Father of our Lord Jesus Christ. You are the Father of all mercies and God of all comfort who comforts us in our affliction so that we may be able to comfort those who are in any affliction for our comfort is abundant through Christ Jesus our Lord who give us His Holy Spirit to abide within His people. Thank You for Your comforter, Abba Father.   **2 Corinthians 1:3-4**

Even though I walk through the valley of the shadow of death, I will fear no evil, for You Lord, are with me. Your rod protects me, and Your staff keeps me close to You, and that is a great comfort to me. Your Holy Spirit connects with me in my spirit and I shall trust   in   you   all   the   days   of   my   life.
Psalm 23:4

Compassionate – is to empathize with those who are suffering and to feel compelled to ease their suffering. It is characteristic for God to show such loving action from the heart.

O Lord, our God, You are gracious and compassionate, and You will not turn Your face away from those who return to You. Just as an earthly father shows compassion to his children, so You, Lord have compassion on those who fear You, because You know us and are mindful that we are but dust. Blessed be Your name, O Most High God.
2 Chronicles 30:9; Psalm 103:13-14

How amazing that You long to be gracious to us, and how utterly amazing that You have compassion on us. You, O Lord, are a God of justice and how blessed we are who long for You. Though the mountains be removed, and the hills be shaken, we know Your loving kindness will not be removed and Your covenant will not be shaken. You are the Lord who has compassion on us. We glorify Your name above all names. **Isaiah 30:18, 54:10**

I have hope in You, Lord, for I know Your loving kindness never ceases, and Your compassion never fails. They are new every morning—not because of any merit in me, but because Your faithfulness is great. Therefore, I am not consumed. If You cause grief, I know You will also have compassion because of Your abundant loving kindness, Your unending compassion. **Lamentations 3:22-23, 31-33**

Creator – *God brought heaven and earth, the universe and all matter and life into existence by the power of His word without using any preexisting matter, and He sustains all that exists.*

Who is like You, Lord of the heavens and the earth? Who, besides, You, could create the heavens and the earth? Who, but You, could make the expanse and separate the waters below from the waters above the expanse by the word of Your power? By Your word, the heavens were made and all their host, for You spoke, and it was so. You commanded and it stood fast as a testimony of You as Creator of all things, seen and unseen. You made the stars and placed them in the sky, and not one is missing. I glorify Your Name in all the earth. **Genesis 1:1, 27; Psalm 33:6, 9**

O my Lord, You formed me in my mother's womb. I give thanks to You for I am fearfully and wonderfully made. All Your works are wonderfully made, and my soul knows it very well. There is nothing too difficult for You. Therefore, I praise You.
 Psalm 139:13-14   Jeremiah 32:17

It is You, Lord God, who created the heavens and stretched them out, who spread out the earth and what comes from it, who gives breath to the people on it and spirit to those who walk on it. **Jeremiah 10:12**

Look around, all peoples of the earth, and see that all things were made through Him, and without Him was not anything made that was made. Therefore, give shouts of praise to the Creator God. **John 1:3**

Father, since the creation of the world, Your invisible attributes, Your eternal power and Your divine nature have been clearly seen and have revealed to all mankind that You are the only true God. The rejection of this truth makes man without excuse before You. Your majesty fills the heavens and the earth, and I praise You for You created me in Your image for Your glory. **Romans 1:20**

Lord Jesus, image of the invisible God, I acknowledge as true that by You all things were created in the heavens and the earth, visible and invisible, whether thrones or dominions or rulers or authorities - all things have been created by You and for You and through You, Lord. All things hold together by the word of Your power. Such knowledge causes me to worship You in truth and in spirit. **Colossians 1:15-17**

Worthy are You, my Lord and my God, to receive glory and honor and power, for You did create all things, and because of Your will, they existed and were created. How magnificent that You would take pleasure in creating such beauty! **Revelation 4:11**

The morning stars sang and shouted for joy when You created the earth. You set the boundaries for the seas where their waves must stop. The sun knows its place and the night its limitations because of the power of Your word. You set the stars in their place and know their number and have given them names. Who but You Creator God, has begotten the drops of dew or sends frost from heaven and the surface of the waters is frozen? You O God, give wisdom to the wise and knowledge to those with understanding for You are their source. You change the times and the seasons. I will worship You for You have created me in Your image. **Job 39, Genesis 1:28**

Christ - *The title, also used as a name, given to Jesus who is also known as the Messiah and Savior and is the second person of the trinity – Father, Son, and Holy Spirit.*

Martha said to Jesus in response to His question if she believed that He was the resurrection and the life, "Yes, Lord, I believe that You are the Christ, the Son of God, who is to come into the world."
John 11:25-27

John explained his purpose for writing the gospel of John, "These things are written that you may believe that Jesus is the Christ, the Son of God, and that believing you may have life in His name."
John 20:30-31

The word which God sent to the children of Israel, preaching peace through Jesus Christ – He is Lord of all – that word you know, was proclaimed throughout all Judea.   **Acts, 10:38**

Discover God and Honor Him for He is our Comforter, He is Compassionate, and He is the Creator. Worship Him in spirit and in truth for He is the Christ!

*****

D

Discover God as

Deity – *synonymous with God; Father, Son, and Holy Spirit. Jesus is the one true God in human form.*

O how I worship You, Jesus, for in You all the fullness of Deity - divine attributes and nature - dwells in bodily form. You are truly Son of God and Son of man.   **Colossians 2:9**

It is good to know that if any man is in Christ Jesus, he is a new creation, the old is gone. All of this is from God who was in Christ Jesus reconciling the world to Himself. What freedom You have given us to serve You since our sins are not counted against us for it was the Father's good pleasure for all the fullness of Deity to dwell in Jesus and to reconcile all things to Himself having made peace through the blood of His cross. What wonderful news we can share with others!
2 Corinthians 5:17-19; Colossians 1:19

Deliverer – *Refers to God whereby He rescues His people from evil and redeems them from sin, death, and the penalty of sin. Jesus is the Great Deliverer of man from sin, bondage, and death.*

Lord, God, even though You spoke these words to Israel, I know they are meant for me as well when You said that when I pass through the waters, You will be with me, and the rivers will not overflow me. You reminded me that when I walk through fire, I will not be burned, and the flame will not consume me, for You are the Lord, my God, the Holy One of Israel, and my Savior who delivers me from outer darkness. Thank You for delivering me from all my woes. **Isaiah 43:2**

Bless the Lord, O my soul, and all that is within me, bless His Holy name! Bless the Lord, O my soul, and forget not any of His benefits, who forgives all my iniquity, who heals all my diseases, who redeems my life from the pit, who crowns me with steadfast love and mercy, who satisfies me with good so that my youth is renewed like the eagles. Bless the Lord, O my soul, for He delivers me. **Psalm 103:1-4**

Lord, I have set my hope on You that I should be delivered from evil, from sin, the penalty of sin, and from the second death, for there is nothing too difficult for You. You have power over death, and I know You will deliver me through Jesus Christ, my Lord, my God, and my Deliverer.
2 Corinthians 1:10

Lord Jesus, You have taught us to pray, "…and forgive us our trespasses as we forgive those who trespass against us. And lead us away from temptation and deliver us from evil." And so, I pray in Your name, Jesus, to be delivered from evil, and I give thanks in Your name for setting me free. **Matthew 6:13**

Lord Jesus, Your power has no equal – even the demons must obey You. You demonstrated such power when you commanded a legion of demons to come out of a demon-possessed man, "Come out of the man, unclean spirit!" And the legion of demons obeyed. The man was clothed and in his right mind. How astounding! Truly You are the great Deliverer. **Mark 5:8**

Dependable – *God can be relied on to do what He says He will do, keep all His promises, and always be who He says He is.*

God is not a man that He should lie, nor a son of man, that He should repent. Has He said, and will He not do it? Or has He spoken, and will He not make it good?   **Numbers 23:19**

You are God, dependable and trustworthy in all You say and do. Heaven and earth will pass away, but Your word will by no means pass away! **Mark 13:31**

Discover God and worship Him for
He is Deity, He is the Deliverer,
and be at peace knowing that
He is dependable!

*****

E

Discover God as

Encourager – *God, through the Holy Spirit inspires courage, spirit, and confidence, and is uplifting.*

You, O Lord, heard my cry. You brought me up out of the pit of destruction; out of the miry clay. I was sinking, but You reached out Your outstretched arm and rescued me. You set my feet firmly upon a rock. You lifted me up. You put a new song in my mouth. You encouraged me; therefore, I will praise You forever. **Psalm 40:2-3**

When my anxious thoughts multiply within me, O my Lord, Your encouragement delights my soul. Who, but You, could do such a marvelous thing? Thank You, Most High God, for You sustain all who stumble, and You raise up all who are bowed down. **Psalm 94:19, 145:14**

I am encouraged and do not fear, for You are with me. I will not anxiously look about me, for You are my God. I look to You for Your strength; for Your help. Surely You will uphold me with Your righteous

right hand. You will never forsake me, mighty God. You encourage me and my soul delights in You.
Isaiah 41:10

"May the God who gives perseverance and encouragement grant you to be of the same mind with one another according to Christ Jesus; that with one accord you may with one voice glorify the God and Father of our Lord Jesus Christ."
Romans15:5-6

Eternal/Everlasting – *God has no beginning, and He has no end to His existence. He is not confined by time since He was before time began and will exist when time, as man knows it, will end. He is everlasting. There is never a time when God was not.*

Look up and be glad, O peoples of the earth. The Lord will reign forever and ever. The eternal God is your dwelling place, and underneath are the everlasting arms. Let us exalt His name forever for His throne is forever and ever.
Exodus 15:18; Deuteronomy 33:27; Psalm 45:6

Who but You, Lord, could utter such profound words when You say, "I lift up My hand to heaven and say, 'As I live forever…' or again when You say, "I am the Alpha and the Omega, who is and who was and who is to come, the Almighty." How I marvel at the One who is high and lifted up; who inhabits eternity; whose name is HOLY. You dwell in the high and

holy place, and You revive the hearts of the contrite and the humble. You are the eternal God and there is none like You.
Deuteronomy 32:40; Revelation 1:8; Isaiah 57:15

Do you not know, O peoples of the earth? Have you not heard? The everlasting God, the Lord, the Creator of the ends of the earth does not become weary or tired. His understanding is inscrutable. He gives strength to the weary. Before the mountains were born, or He did give birth to the earth and the world, even from everlasting to everlasting, He is God, and His loving kindness is from everlasting to everlasting on those who fear Him and His righteousness to children's children. Let us bless the name of God everlasting.   **Isaiah 40:28; Psalm 90:2, 103:17**

Trust in the Lord forever, O peoples, for in God the Lord, we have an everlasting Rock. Your righteousness is an everlasting righteousness, and Your Law is truth and shall never fade away. Give praise and honor to the One who lives forever.
Isaiah 26:4; Psalm 119:142

Lord of the heavens and the earth, Your invisible attributes, namely, Your eternal power and divine nature, have been clearly perceived - ever since the creation of the world, in the things that have been made.   **Romans 1:20**

All that God is exists from everlasting to everlasting. Praise be to the Lord, the God of Israel, from everlasting to everlasting. **Psalm 41:13**

Discover God and give thanks to Him for He is an Encourager and honor His Holy Name for He is Eternal and Everlasting God.

*****

F

Discover God as

Faithful – *God is always true to His promises. He can never draw back from His promises of blessing or of judgment. He is consistently constant, loyal, reliable, steadfast, unwavering, devoted, true, and dependable.*

I believe, O Lord, my God, that You are God - the faithful God who keeps Your covenant and Your loving kindness to a thousand generations with those who love You and keep Your commandments. I know You will cover me with Your pinions and under Your wings, I will find refuge. Your faithfulness is a shield and a buckler to me. I can rest in You for You are faithful even when I am not. Your faithfulness endures to all generations. You have established the earth, and it stands fast. Your kingdom is an everlasting kingdom, and Your dominion endures throughout all generations. You are faithful in all Your words and kind in all Your work, and I adore you.
Deuteronomy 7:9; Psalm 91:4; 119:90, 145:13

Listen O peoples of the earth, "The word of the Lord is upright, and all His work is done in faithfulness."

O Lord God of hosts, who is mighty as You are, O Lord, with Your faithfulness all around you? **Psalm 33:4; 89:8**

Lord, I enter Your gates with thanksgiving and Your courts with praise. I give thanks to You, and I bless Your Holy name for You are good, and Your loving kindness is everlasting and Your faithfulness to all generations. **Psalm 100:5**

Lord Jesus, I await eagerly for You, for You will confirm me to the end - guarantee me - that I would be blameless at Your return. I rejoice to know I shall be in Your presence. I glorify Your name with assurance that You are faithful. Praise be to the living God. **I Corinthians 1:9**

O may the God of peace Himself sanctify me entirely, and may my spirit, and soul, and body be preserved complete without blame at the coming of my lord Jesus Christ. Faithful are You who call me, and I am trusting in You that You will bring it to pass. **1 Thessalonians 5:24**

O my soul, be assured that if I die with Christ Jesus, I shall also live with Him. If I endure, I shall also reign with Him. If I deny Him, He will also deny me. If I am faithless, He remains faithful for He cannot deny Himself. O my soul, know that God does not change; give praise for His steadfast love and His rock-solid faithfulness, O my soul. **2 Timothy 2:13**

Father – *The Father, also known as Yahweh, is the first person of the Trinity. Together with Jesus and the Holy Spirit they, as one God in three persons, were involved in the creation of the universe. The Father longs to be called Father to those who walk away. Jesus referred to the Father over 165 times during His earthly ministry.*

God has said, "I will dwell in them and walk among them. I will be their God, and they shall be My people. I will be a Father to you, and you shall be My sons and daughters," says the LORD Almighty.
2 Corinthians 6:16,18

Jesus said, "Abba, Father, all things are possible for You. Take this cup from Me; nevertheless, not what I will, but what You will." **Mark 14:36**

You did not receive the spirit of bondage again to fear, but you have received the Spirit of adoption by whom we cry out 'Abba, Father.'" **Romans 8:15**

Forgiving – *God removes our sins and our guilt and restores fellowship with Him.*

Bless the Lord, O my soul, and forget none of His benefits - who pardons all my iniquities and heals all my diseases, who redeems my life from the pit, and crowns me with loving kindness and compassion. O my soul, He has dealt graciously with me for He has not dealt with me according to my sins. He has shown mercy in that He has not charged me according to my iniquities. He has removed my transgressions from me. Bless the Lord, O my soul. **Psalm 103:2-3, 10-12**

Heavenly Father, You are the only One who wipes out my transgressions for Your own sake, and You will not remember my sins. Even though my sins are as scarlet, they will be white as snow. How great is Your forgiveness! How trustworthy are Your words! **Isaiah 43:25, 1:18**

Lord God, You made me alive together with You, having forgiven me all my transgressions. You canceled out my debt of sin when You were nailed to the cross. I worship You for You are worthy to receive honor and glory and blessing forever. Thank You for the forgiveness of sins. **Colossians 2:13-14**

Father in heaven, I confess my sins to You and ask for forgiveness from all my unrighteousness. I humble myself before You for You are faithful and righteous to forgive me my sins and to cleanse me from all unrighteousness through the shed blood of Jesus Christ, my Lord and Savior. Though my sins were as scarlet, You made them white as snow. **Isaiah 1:18; 1 John 1:8-9**

Discover God and declare His faithfulness and His forgiveness of those who repent, lavishing His loving kindness upon those who believe.

G

Discover God as

Gentle – *The gentleness of God encircles His love, grace, and mercy, as well as His provisions, protection, disposition, and kindness founded on strength and prompted by love.*

Like a gentle shepherd the Lord will tend His flock. In His arms He will gather the lambs and carry them in His bosom; He will gently lead the nursing ewes. We are His people, the sheep of His pasture. David proclaims, "You have given me the shield of Your salvation and Your right hand has held me up, and Your gentleness has made me strong."
Isaiah 40:11; Psalm 18:35

I hear Your beautiful call to all who are weary and heavy-laden, and You will give them rest. You say, "Take My yoke upon you and learn from Me, for I am gentle and humble in heart, and you will find rest for your souls, for my yoke is easy and my burden is light." I delight to serve in yoke with You, O gentle Son of God, Son of man. **Matthew 11:28-30**

Glorious – *is an attribute applied to God and means exalted excellence and splendor, resplendent in majesty, and of divine attributes. God's infinite, intrinsic worth is worthy of praise, honor, glory, and majesty.*

For You, Lord, are great and highly to be praised. Generation to generation shall declare Your mighty acts. We will stand in awe of the glorious splendor of Your majesty and tell of Your greatness. Men shall speak of the power of Your amazing acts, my God, and my King. We will worship You in the glorious splendor of Your holiness.   **Psalm 145:3-6**

Heavenly father, You have spoken to us in these last days through Your son, whom You appointed heir of all things through whom also You made the world. Jesus is the radiance of Your glory and the exact imprint of Your nature, and He upholds all things by the word of His power. When He made purification of sins, He sat down at Your right hand, Majesty on high, having become as much better than the angels, as He has inherited a more excellent name than theirs **Hebrews 1:3-4**

God – *God is God and there is no other; Father, Son, and Holy Spirit. God is the Most High God, the self-existent One, the Supreme Being, Creator, and principal object of faith and prayer. He is the great I AM.*

Listen O peoples of the earth, "The Lord our God is one God. He is the Rock of our Salvation, our Fortress, and our Deliverer." All the gods of the peoples are worthless idols, but the living God, made the heavens and the earth. You, O Lord God, delivered us from evil so that we shall be with You in Your kingdom for all eternity. Therefore, Let God be exalted! I will give thanks to You, O Lord, and sing praises to Your name.   **2 Samuel 22:2, 47, 50**

The Lord our God, the Lord is one. You are Lord alone. There is only one God and Father of us all. Therefore, we shall love the Lord our God with all our heart and with all our soul and with all our mind and with all our strength.   **Mark 12:29-30**

God describes Himself as, "The Lord, the Lord, the compassionate and gracious God, slow to anger, abounding in love and faithfulness, maintaining love to thousands, and forgiving wickedness, rebellion, and sin."   **Exodus 34:6-7**

Good – *God is virtuous, excellent, and upright. God gives to others, not according to what they deserve but according to His perfect will, His goodness, and His kindness toward them and continues to show His unconditional love to those who do not deserve it. He always does what is right and beneficial.*

Good and upright are You, Lord. You instruct the sinner in the way he should go. You lead the humble in justice. All Your paths are loving kindness and truth. **Psalm 25:8-10**

Oh, taste and see that the lord is good! Blessed is the man who takes refuge in Him. And to the Lord I say, "For You are good and forgiving, abounding in steadfast love to all who call upon You. You are a stronghold in the day of trouble. You know those who take refuge in you.
Psalm 34:8, 86:5; Nahum 1:7

You, O Lord, are ready to forgive and abundant in loving kindness to all who call upon You. Give ear to my prayer and hear my plea. In the day of my trouble, I call upon You for You will answer me and deliver me. **Psalm 86:5-7**

O give thanks unto the Lord, all peoples of the earth, for He is good, for His steadfast love endures forever. He is good to all, and His mercy is over all that He made. **Psalm 136:1, 145:9**

Gracious – *God is a God who gives undeserved or unmerited loving kindness. He sees us as a treasure and delights in us, regardless of our status or behavior.*

Lord God, You are compassionate and gracious, slow to anger, and abounding in loving kindness and truth. I stand in awe of You because You keep loving kindness for thousands. You forgive iniquity, transgressions, and sin. And yet, You will not let the wicked go unpunished. You are gracious, yet just; merciful, yet holy. I bow before You, O gracious God. **Exodus 34:6-7**

You are the God of grace. Your undeserved kindness and mercy are new each morning. Your grace is sufficient for me for Your power is made perfect in weakness. When I am weak, I am made strong in You. Thank You for Your boundless grace.
2 Corinthians 12:9-10

May the Lord bless you and keep you; may the Lord make His face shine on you and be gracious to you; may the Lord lift up His countenance and give you His peace. **Numbers 6:24-26**

Guardian – *God, who is steadfast and faithful, is committed to protect His people from evil.*

Lord God, You are my refuge. O Most High, You are my dwelling place. You have assured me that no evil will befall me, nor will any plague come near my house. You have said, "I will give My angels charge concerning you to guard you in all your ways. They will bear you up in their hands, lest you strike your foot against a stone. **Psalm 91:9-12**

Know this about the Lord, O peoples of the earth, the Lord will keep you from all evil. He will keep your soul. The Lord will guard your going out and your coming in from this time forth and forever.
Psalm 121:7-8

The Lord is my guardian and my keeper. The Lord shall preserve my going out and my coming in. He only is my rock and my salvation. He is my defense; I shall not be moved. In God is my salvation and my glory; the rock of my strength and my refuge, is in God who guards me with His outstretched arm.
Psalm 62:5-6

Guide – *Guide and counsel are similar—God will counsel us with His eye upon us. He will lead us into all truth.*

I look to You, Lord, for You instruct me and teach me in the way I should go. You will counsel me with Your eye upon me. I will trust You with all my heart, and I will not lean on my own understanding. In all my ways, I will acknowledge You for You will make my paths straight. Even though I may make my plans, it is You who guides my steps and directs my stops. Therefore, I delight in You, Lord, as a child delights in his father.   **Psalm 32:8; Proverbs 3:5-6, 16:9**

O Lord, my Redeemer, the Holy One of Israel, You are the Lord my God who teaches me to profit in righteousness, who leads me and guides me in the way I should go. I do not stumble in darkness, for You have brought me into Your marvelous light, You guide me in pleasant places, and my steps are sure. You are the faithful guide to all generations.
Isaiah 48:17-18

Discover God and proclaim the
good news to all nations that
the Most High God is gentle, and
He is glorious. He is God and there is
no other god beside Him. He is good,
He is gracious, He is our Guardian, and
He is our guide who leads us in
all truth.

*****

H

Discover God as

Healer - *God forgives sin and restores to soundness of mind and wellness of body. God heals man's spirit, his mind, and his body.*

Gracious Lord God, You require humility, prayer, devotion, and repentance to receive Your blessing of the healing of our land. We are Your people. We are called by Your name. Help us to humble ourselves to pray, to seek Your face, and to turn from our wicked ways for it is then You will hear from Your throne, You will forgive our sins, and heal our land. You will restore us to Yourself and bless us.
2 Chronicles 7:14

Fear the Lord, O my soul, and be not wise in my own eyes, for it will be healing to my body and refreshment to my bones. O my soul, pay close attention to the words of the Lord. I will keep them close in my heart for His words are life and health for my whole body.   **Proverbs 3:7-8, 4:22**

He was wounded for our transgressions, He was bruised for our iniquities; the chastisement for our peace was upon Him, and by His stripes we are healed. **Isaiah 53:5**

You are the Everlasting God, the Lord, and the Creator of the ends of the earth. You do not become weary or tired. You give strength to the weary and to the one who lacks might, You increase power so that those who wait for You will gain strength; they will mount up with wings like eagles. I thank You for restoring me, for strengthening me, for healing me, **Isaiah 40:28-29, 31**

Jesus, how I marvel that You Yourself bore my sins in Your body on the cross that I might live to righteousness, for it is by Your wounds that I am healed. **1 Peter 2:24**

Your Name is above all names – even more excellent than the angels. I sought Your face when I was sick, and You heard me. I do not know if You healed me directly or if You healed me through medical treatment according to Your will. All I know is that I was sick and now I am healed. Who, but You, Lord, could do such a marvelous thing! **James 5:13-16**

Holy – *God is morally excellent and perfect. He is purity of being in every aspect. He is without sin in thought, word, or deed. He is worthy of complete devotion as the One who is perfect in goodness and*

41

righteousness. Of all the attributes ascribed to God, His holiness is superior—even above His love.

Who is like You, O Lord, among the gods? Who is like You, majestic in holiness, awesome in glorious deeds, and doing wonders? There is no one Holy like You, Lord. There is none besides You. There is no rock like our God. **Exodus 15:11; 1 Samuel 2:2**

Let us worship the Lord in the splendor of His holiness. Let us together ascribe to the Lord the glory due His name. Say among the nations, "The Lord reigns." He is Holy and greatly to be praised.
Psalm 29:2, 96:9-10

As the seraphim call out, "Holy, Holy, Holy, is the Lord of hosts, the whole earth is full of Your glory," I bow before You for You are Most High God - holy and righteous. You are light, and there is no darkness in You. You are pure, and there is no sin in You. I sing praise to You for You are Holy, Holy, Holy, and worthy to receive honor and glory and blessing.
Isaiah 6:3

I am strengthened, uplifted, and encouraged to hear Your words, "Do not fear for I have redeemed you. I have called you by name; you are Mine. When you pass through the waters, I will be with you. When you walk through fire, you shall not be burned for I am the Lord Your God, the Holy One of Israel, Your Savior." Rejoice, O peoples of the earth, the high and exalted One who lives forever, whose name Is HOLY, dwells on a high and holy place and also with the contrite and humble in order to revive the spirit of the lowly and to revive the hearts of the contrite. **Isaiah 43:1, 57:15**

Who is He that is mighty and has done great things for me? Holy is His name. **Luke 1:49**

The heavenly creatures call out, "Holy, Holy, Holy, is the Lord God Almighty, who was, and is, and is to come." Who will not fear You, O Lord, and glorify Your name? For You alone are holy—all the peoples of the nations will come and worship before You for Your righteous acts have been revealed. There is no other god besides You.   **Revelation 4:8, 15:4**

Words spoken to Israel: You shall be holy to Me, for I the Lord am holy.   **Leviticus 20:26**

Exalt the Lord, our God, and worship at His holy hill; for the Lord, our God is holy.   **Psalm 99:9**

Hope – *The confident expectation of what God has promised; the strength of hope is based on God's consistent faithfulness of His character.*

You are my hope, O Lord God, You are my confidence. You pardon all my iniquities; You heal all my diseases; You redeem my life from the pit. You crown me with loving kindness and compassion; You satisfy my years with good things so that my youth is renewed like the eagles. You have not dealt with me according to my sins, but as far as the east is from the west, You have removed my sins. You have shown me compassion for You remember that I am but dust. But You, Lord, are everlasting. You have established Your throne in the heavens and Your sovereignty rules overall. And so, I bless You, Lord, my hope, and my God. **Psalm 71:5, 103**

When I wait for You, Lord, when I hope in You, I will gain strength; I will mount up with wings like eagles, I will run and not be weary; I will walk and not be tired; for You have said, "I know the plans that I have for you - plans for welfare and not for calamity to give you a future and a hope. Therefore, I call upon You for I know You will listen to me.
Isaiah 40:31; Jeremiah 24:11-12

O Most High God, You are the God of hope; may You fill us with all joy and peace in believing that we may abound in hope by the power of the Holy Spirit. Your promises are sure, and our hope is fixed on You who richly supplies us with all good things to enjoy. Blessed be Your name above all else.
Romans 15:13; 1 Timothy 6:17

Discover God and declare Him as healer of mind, body, and spirit. He is holy, and He is the object of a sure hope. Worship Him in the splendor of His holiness.

I

Discover God as

Immortal - *God is not subject to death. He cannot die nor will He ever cease to exist. He is infinite.*

Listen, O peoples, do you not know? Have you not heard? The everlasting God, the Lord, the Creator of the ends of the earth does not become weary or tired. Before the mountains were born, from everlasting to everlasting, He is God. His years are throughout all generations. He is the same, and His years will not end. He is God, Lord of the heavens and the earth and all they contain. Worship Him with a humble heart. **Isaiah 40:28; Psalm 90:2, 102:27**

O sovereign God, King of kings, and Lord of lords, You alone possess immortality and dwell in unapproachable light. Yet, You called us with a holy calling, not according to our works, but according to Your own purpose and grace which was granted us in Christ Jesus from all eternity. This has been revealed to us at Your appearing for You abolished death and brought life and immortality - deathlessness - to light through the gospel - the good news of life eternal through Your victorious death and resurrection.

Thank You for the gift of eternal life. To You be honor and eternal dominion forevermore.
1 Timothy 6:15-16; 2 Timothy 1:10

Lord Jesus, how marvelous that You shall reign as King on earth for a thousand years until You have put all Your enemies under Your feet - the last enemy to be abolished is death. Who but You, sovereign and immortal God, could give eternal life if You were not the immortal, everlasting Father?
1 Corinthians 15:25-26

Immutable – *God is always the same in His nature, character, will and covenant promises. He never changes, and He can never be made to change.*

You do not change. You are like the anchor in a storm; You do not move with the water.
Malachi 3:6

How I marvel, O Lord, that in the beginning You did lay the foundation of the earth and the heavens are the works of Your hands - but they all will become old like a garment, and yet, You are the same, and Your years will not end. I am reminded that You, Jesus, are the same yesterday, today, and forever.
Hebrews 1:10-12, 13:8

Thank You, O Father of lights, for every good and perfect gift that is from You; that comes down to us from above. With You there is no variation or shadow due to change - unlike the shadow on a sun

46

dial that moves with every passing hour. I glorify Your name, for there is none like You, O matchless God. **James 1:17**

Incomprehensible – *Because God is God, He is beyond man's understanding. His ways, His character, and His acts are higher than man's. Man can understand only what God chooses to reveal about Himself.*

Can anyone find out the deep things of God? Tell me if you know - can you know the limit of the Almighty? I do not understand, nor can I comprehend so great a God as You, Lord, but I trust in You with all my heart. I marvel at the depth of the riches and wisdom and knowledge of You. How unsearchable are Your judgments and how inscrutable are Your ways, O Most High God! **Job 11:7; Romans 11:33**

Infinite – *God has no limits or bounds whatsoever in His person, His wisdom, His power, or His dominion. He is limitless.*

Shall the infinite God dwell on the earth and reside in a house built by man's hand? No, even heaven and the highest heaven cannot contain Him! Therefore, I burst forth in praise and worship saying, "Great are You, Lord, and greatly to be praised. Your infinite greatness is unsearchable!" Let us humble ourselves before the great and infinite God and worship him.

1 Kings 8:27; Psalm 145:3

Great is our Lord, and mighty in power; His understanding is infinite. **Psalm 147:5**

Jesus said, "With men this is impossible but with God all things are possible. **Matthew 19:26**

Invisible – *God is Spirit and is unable to be seen by the human eye. No person has seen God in His full divine essence.*

No one has seen God at any time. The only begotten Son, who is in an intimate relationship with the Father, face-to-face with God, has declared Him to us. You, Jesus, are the image of the invisible God. Thank You that we can *see* God through You.
John 1:18; Colossians 1:15

No one has seen God at any time. If we love one another, God the Holy Spirit, abides in us, and His love has been perfected in us. **1 John 4:12**

In the beginning was the Word, and the Word was with God, and the Word was God. He was in the beginning with God. And the Word became flesh and dwelt among us, and we beheld His glory, the glory as of the only begotten of the Father. **John 1:1,14**

Now to the King eternal, immortal, invisible to God who alone is wise, be honor and glory forever and ever. **1 Timothy 1:17**

Discover God as the Lord God immortal, immutable, incomprehensible, infinite, and invisible. Give praise to His matchless name.

*****

J

Discover God as

Jealous – *God is unwilling to share with any other creature what is rightfully and morally His. He is jealous for man meaning that He wants for man what is good and right and perfect. His jealousy is one of protective love to keep His people from idolatry.*

Lord God, I want to be obedient to You in all things for You commanded that we shall have no other gods before You. We shall not worship idols nor anything or anyone above You. You have commanded that we shall not worship or serve them, for You, O Lord our God, are a jealous God. Your name is Jealous for You are a jealous God, and You will not share Your glory, nor give Your glory to another. You will not give Your praise to idols, to graven images. Indeed, Lord, there is nothing worthy of worship except You, for You are God and there is none other. And so, I worship You and You only.
Exodus 20:3-5, 34:14; Isaiah 42:8

Help us, O Most High God, to be mindful not to drink the cup of the Lord and the cup of demons nor to partake of the table of the Lord and the table of demons. Or do we provoke the Lord to be jealous? We are not stronger than He, are we? Grant us discernment that we may worship You in purity and truth, Lord. I know You are jealous *for* Your glory; You are jealous *for* us - You are not jealous **of** anyone for there is no one greater than You.
1 Corinthians 10:21-22

Take heed to yourselves, lest you forget the covenant of the Lord your God which He made with you and make for yourselves a carved image in the form of anything which the Lord your God has forbidden you. For the lord our God is a consuming fire, a jealous God. **Deuteronomy 4: 23-24**

You shall not go after other gods, the gods of the peoples who are all around you for the Lord your God is a jealous God among you.

Jehovah – *means God (YHWH) and is said to be the proper name of God in the Hebrew Bible and the Old Testament. Jehovah also means the eternal One, the unchangeable One, and the One who was, who is, and who is to come.*

You are the Lord Jehovah. I stand in awe to know that when You appeared to Abraham, You said. "I *am* almighty God…." And You spoke to Moses and said

51

to him: "I *am* the Lord. I appeared to Abraham, to Isaac, and to Jacob, as God Almighty, but *by* My name Lord. (Hebrew YHWH, Jehovah). You are Jehovah God, for You are holy, mighty, and powerful. **Genesis 17:1; Exodus 6:2-3**

Behold, Jehovah God, You are my salvation. I will trust and not be afraid for You Lord God are my strength and my song; You have become my salvation. I give You thanks, and I will make known Your wondrous deeds. You are the exalted, and I praise You in song. **Isaiah 12:2-5**

Trust in the Lord forever, for in God the Lord, we have an everlasting Rock - the Rock of ages. **Isaiah 26:4**

Judge – *God can discern the thoughts of man and the intentions of his heart and will hold each man accountable for his actions.*

I will fear You, Lord God of the heavens and the earth, and keep Your commandments for You will bring every act to judgment - everything hidden, whether good or bad. Shall not the Judge of all the earth do right? I therefore desire to have true reverence toward You and that it would be manifested by obedience to You for You alone are the perfect and righteous Judge.
Genesis18:25; Ecclesiastes 12:13-14

The Lord is our Judge, the Lord is our Lawgiver, the Lord is our King; He will save us.   **Isaiah 33:22**

Be assured that God will judge the secrets of men through Christ Jesus, and there is nothing concealed that will not be revealed, nor is there anything hidden that will not be made known, for he is God and His judgments are true. There is no creature hidden from His sight, but all things are naked and open to the eyes of Him to whom we must give an account.
Matthew 10:26; Romans 2:16; Hebrews 4:13

Delight to know that the Lord knows how to rescue the godly from temptation, and He will keep the unrighteous under punishment for the Day of Judgment.   **2 Peter 2:9**

Just – *God is fair and impartial in all His actions, whether He deals with man, angels, or demons. He acts in total equity rewarding righteousness and punishing sin. He will administer justice in accordance with His perfect standard.*

I bless You Lord God, for You are compassionate and gracious, slow to anger and abounding in loving kindness, forgiving iniquity, transgression, and sin; and yet, You will by no means let the guilty go unpunished because You are a just God. I proclaim Your name, O Lord, and ascribe greatness to You. You are the rock! Your work is perfect.
Exodus 34:6-7; Deuteronomy 32:4

The Lord God has shown us what is good; and what does the Lord require of you but to do justly, to love mercy, and to walk humbly with our God.
Micah 6:8

Lord, if I say I have no sin, I deceive myself, and the truth is not in me. If I confess my sins, You are faithful and **just** to forgive me my sins and to cleanse me from all unrighteousness. Thank You, Heavenly Father. **1 John 1:9**

Discover God as the God who is jealous for our good and the blessings He yearns to give us. He also will not share His glory with another. When people commit idolatry against Him, He is Jehovah, the supreme God, He is Judge and will always judge with equity, for God is just. Worship the Lord God Almighty and Him only shall you serve.

*****

K

Discover God as

Kind – *God is kind, and His kindness is demonstrated by being tenderhearted, compassionate, and merciful to the least of these and to those who do not deserve it.*

How precious is Your lovingkindness, O God! Therefore, the children of men put their trust under the shadow of Your wings. **Psalm 36:7**

You, O Most High God, are gracious and full of compassion, slow to anger and great in mercy. You are good to all, and Your tender mercies are over all Your works. You uphold all who fall and raise up all who are bowed down. The eyes of all look expectantly to You, and You give them their food in due season. You open Your hand and satisfy the desire of every living thing.
Psalm 145:8-9, 145:14-15

Lord God of the heavens and the earth, because Your lovingkindness is better than life, my lips shall praise You. I will bless you while I live; I will lift up my hands in Your name. **Isaiah 63:3-4**

King – *Expresses that God is the sovereign ruler of the universe, and Christ as the Son of God is the head and governor of the church. Jesus is King of kings. All authority has not been delegated to God – He is the supreme authority.*

In the morning I cry out to You for help, my King, and my God. I will order my prayer to You and eagerly watch, King of glory. And who is the King of Glory? The Lord strong and mighty, the Lord of hosts, He is the King of glory. Therefore, I will wait in confidence. **Psalms 5:2, 24:7-8**

God of all the heavens and the earth who will bring about His reward at the proper time. He who is called the Blessed, Sovereign, the King of kings and Lord of lords. He alone possesses immorality and dwells in unapproachable light; whom no man has seen or can see. To Him be honor and eternal dominion! I bow before you and worship You, O my King.
1 Timothy 6:15-16

An inscription written in Greek, Latin, and Hebrew and nailed to the cross above Jesus' head that read, "THIS IS JESUS THE KING OF THE JEWS."
Matthew 27:37

Who could imagine waging war against the Lamb? The ten-nation federation will rise up, but You, O Lamb, will overcome them because You are Lord of lords and King of kings and there is no one like You, O mighty King. You will smite the nations; You will

rule them with a rod of iron; You will tread the wine press of the fierce wrath of God, the Almighty. And on Your robe and on Your thigh is written the name "KING OF KINGS AND LORD OF LORDS."
 Revelation 17:14, 19:16

Discover God as Kind and as King. Sing a song of praise with a grateful heart to the King of kings who shows kindness, compassion, and mercy to all the people of the nations.

*****

$\mathcal{L}$

Discover God as

Light - *Light is always contrasted with darkness—God is the absolute Sovereign who rules over the darkness, and the powers of evil. Jesus is the Light of the world.*

You, O Lord, are my light and my salvation; whom shall I fear? You are the stronghold of my life; whom shall I dread?   **Psalms 27:1**

You are the Light of the world, and Your testimonies are pure and wonderful. Therefore, my soul observes them. The unfolding of Your words gives light and understanding, and I love it. You, Lord, are an everlasting light. You are my glory. I have no need for the sun or for the moon, for You are my everlasting Light.   **Psalms 119:129-130**

Jesus, You Yourself said, "I am the Light of the world; he who follows Me shall not walk in darkness but shall have the light of life." What an awesome promise! You are an amazing God, and there is no one like You! I worship You for You are light and in

You there is no darkness. You have called me, even me, out of darkness into Your marvelous light.
John 8:12; 1 John 1:5

Limitless – *God is immeasurable; He is without limits or boundaries. He is not confined by time nor is He stifled by endless space.*

Who commands the sun to shine or not to shine? Who above stretches out the heavens and tramples down the waves of the sea? Who makes the Bear, Orion, and the Pleiades? Who does great things, unfathomable, and wondrous works without number? I know, Lord of the heavens and the earth, that You alone are He. I know You can do all things, and there is nothing that can thwart Your purpose, and so I worship You for You are limitless in Your nature.
Job 9:7-10, 42:2

Bless the Lord, O my soul, for You are my God, a very great God. You are clothed with splendor and majesty. You stretch out heaven like a tent curtain. You make the clouds Your chariot, and You walk upon the wings of the wind. You make the winds Your messengers and flaming fire Your ministers. Your power and majesty are without limitation, O my great and awesome God. There is nothing too difficult for You. Time does not limit You; for a day is as a thousand years, and a thousand years as one day. I praise You Lord of all.   **Psalms 104:1-4**

Listener – *The power of prayer is not in the one who asks; it is in the One who listens.*

Heavenly Father, when I call upon You, I know You hear me and will answer me. When I am in distress, I cry out to You, and You hear my cry. Our iniquities have made a separation between us and You, O Holy God, and because of our sins You have hidden Your face from us so that You do not hear. But behold, Lord, Your hand is not so short that it cannot save, neither is Your ear so dull that You cannot hear our cry to You. Because of Your grace and mercy, You have delivered us from the bondage of our sin. I praise You, my Lord, and my God.
Psalms 92:15, 106:44-45; Isaiah 59:1-2

Give ear O Lord, to my prayer and listen to the voice of my deep and earnest prayers. In the day of trouble, I will call upon You, for You will answer me. There is no one like You among the gods, O Lord; nor are there any works like Yours. You hear my call and rescue me.   **Psalms 86:6-8**

O how I am assured that when I call upon You, Lord God, and come and pray to You that You will listen for You have said so. And again, I am confident that if I seek You, I will find You when I search for you with my whole heart. Thank You for Your promises for You are not a god who lies.   **Jeremiah 29:12-13**

Now this is the confidence that we have in Him, that if we ask anything according to His will, He hears us. And if we know that He hears us, whatever we ask, we know that we have the petitions that we have asked Him. **1 John 5:14-15**

Longsuffering – *God patiently endures man's sin and His righteous anger against sin is slow to be kindled, but He will not hold His anger forever.*

Lord God, You are merciful and just, compassionate, and gracious. You are slow to anger and abounding in steadfast love, forgiving our iniquities and transgressions. And yet, You will by no means let the guilty go free. **Exodus 34:6; Numbers 14:18**

Lord God, You are merciful and gracious, slow to anger, and abounding in mercy. You will not always strive with us, nor will You keep Your anger forever. You have not dealt with us according to our sins, nor punished us according to our iniquities. Thank You that You are patient and merciful. **Psalm 103:8-10**

Lord God Almighty, how gracious and merciful You are! You are longsuffering and great in loving kindness. You are good to all, and Your mercies are over all Your works. The godly ones shall bless You; they shall speak of Your glory and talk of Your power; to make known to man Your mighty acts and the glory of Your kingdom. **Psalm 145:8-12**

Beloved, do not let this one fact escape your notice - with the Lord, one day is as a thousand years, and a thousand years are as one day. He is not slow in His promise to return as some count slowness, but He is patient and longsuffering, not wishing that any should perish, but for all to come to repentance before the great and terrible day of the Lord.
2 Peter 3:8-9

Lord - YHWH or *Jehovah is the proper name of the eternal God and Creator of the heavens and the earth and means supreme master.*

God spoke to Moses, "I am the Lord (Jehovah); and I appeared to Abraham, Isaac, and Jacob, as God Almighty, but by My name, Lord, I did not make known to them." We may be certain that God alone, whose name is the Lord, is the Most High over all the earth.   **Exodus 6:3; Psalm 83:18**

You are my salvation. I will trust and not be afraid, for You Jehovah God, are my strength and my song; You have become my salvation.   **Psalm 12:2**

Lord Jesus, You are awesome! Though You existed in the form of God - being of the same nature and essence of God - You did not exploit Your position to Your own advantage! How amazing that You would empty Yourself without surrendering any attributes of Deity to take on the limitations of humanity while You were on earth! No wonder God highly exalted

You and bestowed on You the name that is above every name that at the name of Jesus, every knee should bow - of those in heaven and on earth and under the earth, and every tongue confess, "You are LORD" to the glory of God the Father.
Philippians 2:5-11

Do you not know that if you confess with your mouth Jesus as LORD and believe in your heart that God raised Him from the dead, you shall be saved? Do you not also know that if we live, we live for the Lord, or if we die, we die for the Lord? Therefore, whether we live or whether we die, we are the Lord's. It is for this reason that Christ Jesus died and lived again that He might be Lord both of the dead and of the living.   **Romans 10:9, 14:9**

Loving - *God's love moves Him to the laying down of His own life for the salvation of others. It is His love that causes Him to desire the highest good for man, and it is not based upon the worth, response, or merit of man.*

Father God, You are ready to forgive and abundant in loving kindness to all who call upon You. Therefore, I praise you for Your love never fails.
Psalms 86:5

How we can delight to know that God demonstrates His love for us in that while we were yet sinners, Christ died for us! For God so loved the world that he

gave His only begotten Son that whoever believes in Him should not perish but have everlasting life. Beloved, let us love one another, for love is from God. Anyone who does not love, does not know God, for God is love.
John 3:16; Romans 5:8; 1 John 4:7

Are we not convinced that neither death, nor life, nor angels, nor principalities, nor things present, nor things to come, nor powers, nor height, nor depth, nor any other created thing shall be able to separate us from His love, which is in Christ Jesus, our Lord. To God be glory and honor now and forevermore.
Romans 8:38-39

Father God, You are rich in mercy, and ready to forgive and abundant in loving kindness to all who call upon You. Because of Your great love with which You loved us - even when we were dead in our sins - You made us alive together with Christ and raised us up with Him and seated us with You in the heavenly places in Christ Jesus. To You belong glory and honor and praise for all eternity.
Ephesians 2:4-5

O precious one, please come to know and believe the love which God has for us because God is love, and the one who abides in love abides in God, and God abides in him. **1 John 4:16**

Discover God as the Light, because He is Limitless, He is a Listener, He is longsuffering, He is LORD, and He is loving. Honor Him for He is the Light of the world and without Him, we would be in darkness. God is love and thereby, learn what it means to love others as He has loved us.

*****

M

Discover God as

**Merciful** - _God is merciful and shows this by not giving the punishment to those who deserve it._

Lord God of the heavens and the earth, make me know Your ways, teach me Your paths. Lead me in Your truth and teach me, for You are my God, the God of my salvation, and for You I wait. Remember, O Lord, Your compassion and Your mercy and Your loving kindness. Forgive me all my sins for Your name's sake. Who is a God like You, who pardons iniquity because of Your tender mercy? How grateful I am that You do not retain Your anger forever because You delight in steadfast love and mercy. Blessed be Your Holy name.
Psalms 25:4-6; Micah 7:18

Listen, O peoples of the earth, seek the Lord while He may be found, call upon Him while He is near. Return to the Lord, and He will have mercy for He will abundantly pardon us from our sins. Thank You, Merciful God, that You do pardon our sins.
Isaiah 55:6-7

Blessed be You, God, and Father of our Lord Jesus Christ, who according to Your great mercy has caused us to be born again to a living hope through the resurrection of Jesus Christ from the dead to an inheritance which is imperishable and undefiled, and kept in heaven for us. We bless You, O Merciful God.   **1 Peter 1:3-4**

Messiah - *The name chosen by God for Jesus, the Christ, the Messiah, and the Savior. The Lord is salvation - the One whom God sent to save people from their sins and to be their king.*

How amazing, Jesus, when the magi from the east arrived in Jerusalem and asked where the King of the Jews was born, that Herod was troubled and summoned all the chief priests and scribes and inquired, "Where is the Messiah to be born?" and how amazing their answer, "In Bethlehem." Truly, Lord Jesus, You are the Christ, the Messiah, and I worship You.   **Matthew 2:4**

Let's join with Andrew when he discovered a life-changing fact. Let us say the words he said to his brother, Peter, "We have found the Messiah!" And he brought him to Jesus. And listen to the words of the woman at the well when she responded to Jesus, "I know that Messiah is coming (He who is called Christ); when that One comes, He will declare all things to us." Jesus replied, "I who speak to you am

He." Let us worship Jesus, the Messiah, and exult His name together! **John 1:41**

Mighty – *God is infinite in power, strength and might.*

You, O Most High God, are wise in heart and mighty in strength. Who could defy You without harm? You have might to remove mountains when You overturn them in Your anger—You shake the earth from its pillars. If it is a matter of power, You are the strong One. **Job 9:4-5, 19, 23:6**

Great are You Lord and worthy to be praised for You are mighty in power, You lift up the humble, and Your understanding is infinite. You are mighty and the Lord of hosts is Your name. You are my God and I worship You. **Psalm 145:5-6; Jeremiah 50:35**

God is opposed to the proud, therefore let us humble ourselves under the mighty hand of God, so that at the proper time, He may exalt us. Let us cast our cares and anxieties on Him because He cares for us. **1 Peter 5:5-6**

Discover God for His mercy and because of His mercy, He does not give sinners what they deserve; He is the long-awaited Messiah who saves; and He is mighty indeed for the good of all people.

*****

$\mathcal{N}$

Discover God as

Near – _God is close to the broken-hearted; He draws near to His people._

The righteous cry and You hear and deliver us out of our troubles. You, O Lord, are near to the brokenhearted, and You save those who are crushed in spirit. You redeem the souls of Your servants, and none of us who take refuge in You will be condemned for You are a God who is near to all who call upon You in truth. Because You are not a God far off, we cry out to you, and we bless Your Holy name forever and ever.
Psalms 34:17-18, 22, 145:18

I need not be anxious for anything, for You, O Lord, are nearby. In everything by prayer and supplication with thanksgiving I will let my requests be made known to You. And Your peace which surpasses all understanding will keep my heart and my mind in You, Christ Jesus. **Philippians 4:5-9**

I know that if I draw near to You, Lord God, You will draw near to me, and so I praise You. **James 4:8**

Discover God as you draw near to Him with a joyful heart, because He is not a God far off.

*****

O

Discover God as

Obedient – _Jesus portrayed the supreme example of obedience to the heavenly Father when He gave Himself as the ultimate sacrifice for the forgiveness of sins. Jesus said, "Not My will, but Your will be done._

Lord Jesus, I marvel that You existed in the form of God - being the exact imprint of His nature - yet You did not regard equality a thing to hold on to or to exploit for Your own personnel gain. How amazing that you would empty Yourself and become like man, and while in human form, become obedient to death on a cross. I cannot imagine hearing Your prayers said with loud cries and tears to Your Father - the One able to save You from death - and yet, You learned obedience from the things You suffered. How it must have grieved Your Father to see His Son suffer so, and yet, how it must have pleased Him to see Your obedience for the sake of sinners. I praise You, O Lamb of God, for You alone are worthy to receive honor and glory and blessing.
Philippians 2:8; Hebrews 5:7-8

I stand in awe of You, Jesus, that You would be so obedient to Your heavenly Father that you would say, "If it be possible let this cup of suffering pass from Me; yet not as I will, but as You will." What great love You have for Your heavenly Father that whatever He commands, You obediently so do. I worship You, Son of the Most High for You do all things for our good and for Your glory.
Matthew 26:39

I look at the one man's disobedience and see the many were made sinners; and yet, through the obedience of the One, Jesus, many will be made righteous. What a gift You wrought through Your obedience - the gift of eternal life. I praise and give thanksgiving to You throughout all eternity.
Romans 5:19

Omnipotent – *God is all powerful; having unlimited power and authority. He can accomplish all He has purposed without use of any source beyond Himself.*

Lord God, I believe that You can do all things and no purpose of Yours can be thwarted for You are all powerful and there is no other god besides You. For by the word of Your mouth, the heavens and all their hosts were made. Let all the inhabitants in the world stand in awe of You. You speak and it is done. You are to be greatly praised! **Job 42:2; Psalm 33:6-9**

You have made the earth by Your power, You have established the world by Your wisdom, and have stretched out the heavens at Your discretion. When You speak, there is a multitude of waters in the heavens, and You cause the vapors to ascend from the ends of the earth. You make lightning for the rain, and You bring the wind out of Your treasuries. I stand in awe of You. **Jeremiah 10:12-13**

Once God has spoken; twice we have heard this; that all power belongs to God. It is You who made the heavens and the earth by Your great power and by Your outstretched arm! Nothing is too difficult for You. **Psalms 62:11; Jeremiah 32:17**

How amazing that our God upholds the universe by the word of His power. Who but You is worthy to make purification for sins and to sit down at the right hand of the majesty on high? **Hebrews 1:3**

Lord of the heavens and the earth, You are the Alpha and the Omega who is and who was and who is to come, the Almighty. You are the beginning and the end of all things - seen and unseen. We praise You with the hosts of heaven who say, "Give praise to our God all who fear Him." Their voices, like mighty peals of thunder say, "Hallelujah! For the Lord our God, the Almighty, reigns." **Revelation 19:5-6**

Omnipresent - *God is always present everywhere in all the universe in the totality of His character.*

O Lord, You are the One who goes ahead of me; You will be with me. You will not fail or forsake me. I will not fear or be dismayed. You are an ever-present help in times of trouble, and I delight in You for You are faithful God.   **Deuteronomy 31:8**

Nothing is hidden from Your ever-present eyes. Where can I hide from Your Spirit or where could I flee from Your presence? If I ascend to heaven, You are there. If I make my bed in Sheol, You are there. If I ride the winds of the morning and dwell in the remotest part of the sea, even there Your hand will lead me. You have said, "Can a man hide himself in hiding places, so I do not see him? Do I not fill the heavens and the earth?" You, O Most High God, are an ever-present God; One who is near and not far off. I joy to know there is no distance or time that is beyond Your omnipresence.
Psalm 139:7-10; Jeremiah 23:23-24

For certain the eyes of the Lord are in every place, watching the evil and the good. His eyes run to and fro over the entire earth to give strong support to those whose heart is completely devoted to Him.
Proverbs 15:3; 2 Chronicles 16:9

Thank You, Lord Jesus that You are with me - even to the end of the ages. Thank You that You have not forsaken me or left me as an orphan. Wherever I may go, I know You are with me, and for that comforting assurance, I give You thanksgiving.   **Matthew 28:20**

Omniscient – *God has perfect knowledge of everything – all actual and all possible things; past, present, and future.*

O peoples of the earth, do you know the balancing of the clouds, the wondrous works of Him who is perfect in knowledge? Listen to what the psalmist says, "O Lord, You have searched me and known me! You know when I sit down and when I rise up. You discern my thoughts from afar. You search out my path and my lying down and are acquainted with all my ways. Even before a word is on my tongue, behold, O Lord, You know it altogether. Such knowledge is too wonderful for me; it is high; I cannot attain it." You, O Lord, have perfect
knowledge of everything past, present, and future and I worship You, for You are a great God.
Job 37:16; Psalm 139:1-6

One – *God is one God who exists in three divine persons: the Father who is revealed in the Old Testament to be Creator, Lord, Father and Judge; the Son, who in the New Testament, is Jesus and Savior, and is the exact image of the Father in body form; and the Holy Spirit who is the Spirit of the Father and the Son and indwells all believers*
.

"Hear, O Israel. The Lord our God, the Lord is one. You shall love the Lord your God with all your heart and with all your soul and with all your might." **Deuteronomy 6:4**

When Jesus had been baptized by John, He came up immediately from the water; and the heavens were opened to Him, and He saw the Spirit of God descending like a dove and alighting upon Him. And suddenly a voice came from heaven, saying, "This is my beloved Son, in whom I am well pleased." Lord, thank You for letting us hear the voice of the Father, seeing the Holy Spirit as a dove, and seeing Jesus in human flesh. I am filled with awe at Your glory. **Matthew 3:16-17.**

Jesus said, "I and My Father are one." **John 10:30**

There is one body and one Spirit, just as you were called in one hope of your calling; one Lord, one faith, one baptism; one God and Father of all, Who is above all, and through all, and in you all. **Ephesians 4:4-6**

Discover God through the perfect obedience of Jesus Christ, His only begotten Son. Be in awe of His omnipotence and be amazed at His presence everywhere in the entire universe at the same time. Give praise to the One who has perfect knowledge in all actual and all possible things since the beginning of time. Worship the one true God and Father of us all.

*****

P

Discover God as

Patient – *God is compassionate and gracious, slow to anger, and abounding in steadfast love.*

You, O Most High God, are a God who forgives, You are gracious and compassionate, slow to anger, and abounding in loving kindness. You do not abandon or forsake the sinner who turns away from You. The many times You rescue us when we cry out to You is evidence of Your immense patience. Your anger is but for a moment, and Your favor is for a lifetime. Weeping may tarry for the night, but with You, a shout of joy comes with the morning.
Nehemiah 9:17, 28; Psalms 30:5; Psalm 145:8

Listen, O peoples of the earth, the Lord God will not keep His anger forever. Take heart, beloved, He has not dealt with us according to our sins for as high as the heavens are above the earth, so great is His loving kindness toward those who fear Him. He is patient with us, not wanting anyone to perish, but everyone to come to repentance. Therefore, let us exalt His great name!   **Psalms 103:8-10**

Did you not know, O sons and daughters, the Lord is patient toward us not wishing for any to perish, to die without hope, but for all to come to repentance and live? Receive His blessing with a grateful heart. **Joel 2:13-14; 2 Peter 3:9**

Perfect – *God is complete, whole, totally righteous, holy, the utmost of the highest beings, sinless, and without spot or blemish.*

As for God, His way is perfect; the word of the Lord is proven; He is a shield to all who trust in Him. **Psalm 18:30**

Be perfect, therefore, as your Heavenly Father is perfect. Lord God, You possess all perfections. Lord, when I consider the sun, the moon, the stars, and all the splendor of all Your creation in its perfection, which you ordained, what is man that You are mindful of him? **Matthew 5:48; Psalm 8:3-4**

Personal – *God knows every human being by my name. He understands our thoughts, our hearts, and knows everything about us. God relates to every individual in such a way that is unique to each person.*

You, my Lord, and my God. You are a personal God because You do not see me as man sees me. Man looks at my outward appearance, but You Lord, look at my heart. You light my lamp and illumine my darkness. You have searched me, and You know me. You know when I sit down and when I rise up. You know and understand my thoughts. You are intimately acquainted with all my ways. Even before a word is on my tongue, You know it already. You know the number of hairs on my head. You exult over me with joy. You rejoice over me with singing. You are quiet in Your love and rejoice over me with shouts of joy for I am your child, and You are my God.

1 Samuel 16:7; Psalms 18:28-29; 139:1-4; Zephaniah 3:17; Matthew 10:30

Powerful – *God is strong, mighty, and with His powerful hand He led His people out of Egypt with mighty signs and wonders. His voice is powerful - like the roar of many waters - He is majestic.*

Lord of the heavens and the earth, You are an amazing God and there is no other god like You. Your great power was displayed to Your people Israel and to the Egyptians when you swept back the sea with a strong east wind all night and led Your people through on dry land between walls of water. I wonder if I were among them and saw your great power as they did, if I too would fear You, Lord, and be in awe of You. I cannot imagine anyone being indifferent to such a display of power, O Mighty and powerful God. **Exodus 14:21, 31**

God has spoken once, twice I have heard this: That power belongs to God and nothing and anyone could triumph over You. **Psalm 62:11**

O Lord God of hosts, who is like You, O mighty and powerful Lord? You rule the swelling waves of the sea, and when they rise, You quell them. The heavens are Yours and the earth and all they contain for You have made them. You have a strong arm; Your hand is mighty. Who in the skies compares to You, Lord? Who among the sons of the mighty is like You?
I ascribe to You the glory and strength due Your name, O most powerful God of all creation. **Psalms 89:6, 8, 11, 13**

It is You, O Lord, who made the earth by the power of Your word. You established the world by Your wisdom, and by Your understanding, You stretched out the heavens. When You speak, there is a tumult of waters in the heavens, and You cause the clouds to ascend from the end of the earth. You make lightning for the rain and bring forth the wind from Your storehouses. Who is like You? There is no other god, but You. All the gods of the peoples are worthless idols, but You made the heavens and the earth by the word of Your might. **Jeremiah 51:15-16**

Let the name of You, O God, be blessed forever and ever for wisdom and power belong to You. It is You who change the times and the seasons; You remove kings and establish kings; You give wisdom to the wise and knowledge to those of understanding. You reveal profound and hidden things; You know what is

in the darkness, and the light dwells with You. To You alone, O God, I give thanks and praise.
Daniel 2:20-21

Father, I pray that the eyes of my heart may be opened so that I may know what is the hope of my calling, what are the riches of glory of Your inheritance in the saints, and what is the surpassing greatness of Your power toward those who believe in Christ Jesus who is seated at Your right hand in honor and sovereign power in the heavenly places - far above all rule and authority and power and dominion. **Ephesians 1:18-21**

Protector – *God defends and guards His people from all evil. He is like a shield because He care for us.*

As for me, the nearness of God is my good. He is my Protector. I have made the Lord God my refuge that I may tell of all His works. I delight to praise His Name. **Psalm 73:28**

He who dwells in the shelter of the Most High will abide in the shadow of the Almighty. I will say to the Lord, "My refuge and my fortress, My God, in whom I trust for You deliver me from the snare of the evil ones. You cover me as with Your pinions, and under Your wings as it were, I seek refuge. Your faithfulness is a shield and a protection. You rescue me and keep me. To God be the glory for great things You have done." **Psalms 91:1-4**

I will not be afraid of the terror by night or the destruction that lays waste in the day for I know nothing evil shall approach me for I have the Lord as my refuge, the Most High is my hiding place, my shield, and my protector. **Psalm 91:5-10**

O Lord, where do I look for help and protection? My help comes from You, Lord, maker of heaven and earth. You will not allow my foot to slip. You are my keeper, my protector, and You do not slumber or sleep. You are always attentive to me and keep me from dangers. You will protect me from all evil. You keep my soul. You guard my going out and my coming in from this time and forevermore.
Psalms 121

Discover God who is Patient; be in awe of His perfection, revel in His Personal connection He offers us, rest in the truth that God is Powerful and able to deliver us from all evil; and feel safe to know He is our Protector. Give praise to the Lord God Almighty.

*****

Q

Qualified – *God is all-knowing, all-powerful,* supremely *good, and He sovereignly reigns over the entire universe, over everyone, and over everything. Jesus, God's Son, is qualified to be the Savior of the world because He alone lived a sinless life as a human being. He died for the sins of the world and was raised again. The Holy Spirit is qualified to make us more like Jesus Christ. He renews the minds of believers by convicting believers of sin and leading them to repentance.*

Qualified – I am the Lord, and there is no other. There is no God besides Me. I will gird you, though you have not known Me. That they may know from the rising of the sun to its setting that there is none besides Me. I am the Lord, and there is no other. **Isaiah 45:5-6**

You shall love the Lord your God with all your heart with all your soul, and with all your strength. **Deuteronomy 6:5**

For God so loved the world that He gave His only begotten Son that whoever believes in Him will not perish but have everlasting life. *John 3:16*

Behold! The Lamb of God who takes away the sin of the world. **John 1:29**

He who believes in the Son has everlasting life; and he who does not believe the Son shall not see life, but the wrath of God remains on him. **John 3:36**

But the Helper, the Holy Spirit, whom the Father will send in My name will teach you all things and bring to your remembrance all things that I said to you. **John 14:6**

But when the Helper comes, whom I shall send to you from the Father, the Spirit of truth who proceeds from the Father, He will testify of Me. **John 15:26**

*****

R

Discover God as

Radiant – *A brilliance emanating from a glorious source of light. Jesus is the radiance of God's glory - not a reflected brightness like the light of the moon; instead, this is an inherent brightness like a ray from the sun.*

Jesus, You are the radiance of God's glory; the exact image of His person revealing the brightness of God's glory to humanity. O that all would taste and see that You are good and be blessed to trust in You. You are greatly to be praised!
 Hebrews 1:3; Psalm 34:8

I look to You, Lord Jesus, for You are the Light of the world, and those who follow You shall not walk in darkness but will have the light of life. In You, Jesus, is life, and the life was the light of men.
John 1:4, 8:12

Redeemer – *God saves His people from slavery to sin, and bondage of the oppressed.*

Heavenly Father, from a broken heart, Job proclaimed, "I know that my Redeemer lives, and at the last He will take His stand on the earth." What blessed assurance that You are my Rock and my Redeemer as well. **Job 19:25**

In You, Jesus, we have redemption through Your blood, the forgiveness of our sins according to the riches of Your grace which You lavished upon us. Your love and grace are extravagantly poured out on us. Thank You for redeeming me; for delivering me from sin; and to worship You with a pure heart. **Ephesians 1:7**

We have all sinned and fall far short of Your glory, O Most High God, but through the redemption that is in Christ Jesus, we are justified by Your grace through faith in the Redeemer as the only means of salvation. **Romans 3:23**

Refuge – *God is a shelter who protects us from danger, distress, or calamity; a stronghold who protects by His strength; He is a sanctuary of safety inaccessible to the enemy.*

God, You are our refuge and our strength - a very present help in trouble. You are a strong tower and the righteous run into it and are safe. Blessed be the name of our God. **Psalm 46:1; Proverbs 18:10**

My soul, wait in silence for God only, for my hope is from Him. You only are my rock and my salvation, my stronghold; I shall not be shaken. On You, O God, my salvation, and my glory rest. You are the rock of my strength, my refuge. Trust in Him at all times, O people; pour out your hearts before Him— God is a refuge for us. He is our refuge and our rock. **Psalms 62:5-8**

I will trust in the Lord forever. For in God the Lord, I have an everlasting Rock. O come, let us sing to the Lord! Let us shout joyfully to the Rock of our salvation. Let us delight in Him. **Isaiah 26:4, Psalm 95:1**

Righteous – *God is always perfect in all He does. He always does the right thing, and whatever He does is right. He has never sinned in thought, word, or deed. He is absolute perfection, and His purposes and plans are always consistent with His character.*

You, Lord, are righteous. You love righteousness. Your righteousness reaches to the highest heaven. You have done great and marvelous things. O God, who is like You? Your judgments are upright, and You have commanded Your testimonies in righteousness and exceeding faithfulness. You

always judge in righteousness and Your commandments are righteous forever.
Psalms 11:7, 71:19, 119:137-138, 144, 172

For the word of the Lord is right, and all His work is done in truth. He loves righteousness and justice; the earth is full of the goodness of the Lord. Let all the earth fear the Lord; let all the inhabitants of the world stand in awe of Him.   **Psalm 33:4-5,8**

Lord Jesus, You have renewed me and have made me new in the likeness of God, created in righteousness and holiness of the truth, and so it is for anyone who is in you, Christ Jesus. He is a new creature of righteousness - the old has passed away. How amazing to think that You, righteous Son of the Most High, who loved me and gave Yourself up for me, should be the very One who dwells within me. What grace! Our righteousness cannot come through the law, but only through Your death and resurrection. You have clothed me in Your robe or righteousness. What amazing grace!
Ephesians 4:23-24

Rock - A rock is a symbol of stability, permanence, strength, dependability, and steadfastness. A rock stresses the unchanging nature of God.

The Lord is my rock, my fortress, and my deliverer; my God is my Rock in whom I take refuge, my shield and the horn of my salvation, my stronghold.
Psalms 18:2

My soul, wait silently for God alone, for my expectation is from Him. He only is my rock and my salvation; he is my defense; I shall not be moved. In God is my salvation and my glory; the rock of my strength and my refuge is in God.   **Psalm 62:5-6**

Discover God through the radiance Jesus revealed to humanity for in His human form, Jesus remained the exact imprint of the Father; be assured that our Redeemer lives and intercedes for us before His Father.; Have confidence that God is our Refuge and our strength; He is our Rock and shall never be moved. Give praise to the Righteous One who has clothed us in His righteousness. He is our firm foundation.

*****

S

Discover God as

Savior – _God determined in eternity past to save His people from their sin - from its penalty, its power and one day from its very presence through His beloved son, Jesus Christ, the Savior of the world._

Lord God, You say, "Lift up your eyes to the sky, then look to the earth beneath; for the sky will vanish like smoke and the earth will wear out like a garment, and its inhabitants will die in like manner, but My salvation shall be forever." Thank You, O Most High, that we can be confident in You as our everlasting Savior. **Isaiah 51:6, 8**

My Lord and Savior Jesus Christ, truly we all, like sheep, have gone astray; each one of us has turned his own way, but the Lord laid on You the sins of us all. You take away the sin of the world. You are the Lamb of God, our Savior. **Isaiah 53:6**

How wonderful to celebrate the day You were indeed born the Savior of the world, who is Christ the Lord. I have fixed my hope on You, my Savior Christ Jesus, because You abolished death, brought life and immorality to light through the gospel - for from the offspring of David, according to the promise, God has brought to Israel a Savior who is Jesus Christ the Lord. I look with great expectation for the appearing of the glory of our great God and Savior Christ Jesus. **Luke 2:11; John 4:42; Acts 13:23; 1 Timothy 4:10; Titus 2:13**

We know that if while we were still Your enemies, we were reconciled to You through the death of Your Son, how much more shall we be saved by His life? **Romans 5:10**

I believe and bear witness that You, Father, have sent Your Son as Savior of the world, and whoever confesses that Jesus is Your Son, abides in You and You abide in us. **1 John 4:14**

Beloved, do you not know that when the kindness of God our Savior and His love for mankind appeared, He saved us - not on the basis of deeds which we have done in righteousness, but according to His mercy, by the washing of regeneration - the cleansing of the new birth - and renewing of the Holy Spirit - the continued renewing by the Spirit - whom He poured out upon us through Jesus Christ our Savior, so that being justified by His grace we might be made heirs according to the hope of eternal life? Salvation is a gift of God's grace, not as a reward for any worthwhile acts we may have done. Let us praise the Father, Son, and Holy Spirit. **Titus 3:4-7**

Self-Existent – *God depends on nothing for His existence beyond Himself. He has no beginning or end; He has no origin or creation point.*

Lord Jesus, when You prayed to Your Father with these words, "Father glorify Me together with Yourself with the glory which I had with You before the world was," I marvel at the love and fellowship and glory shared between the Father and You even long before creation.   **John 17:5**

Hear, O peoples of the earth, "For by God all things were created, in heaven and on earth, visible and invisible, whether thrones or dominions or rulers or authorities – all things were created through Him and for Hin. He is before all things, and in Him all things hold together.   **Colossians 1:16-17**

Self-Sufficient – *God possesses within Himself every quality, ability, and supernatural command with never-ending measure. Every attribute is His without end. God wants for nothing and lacks nothing. He is complete.*

Do you not know? Have you not heard? The Everlasting God, the Lord, the Creator of the ends of the earth does not become weary or tired. He depends on nothing for His existence. For just as the Father has life in Himself, even so He gave to the Son also

to have life in Himself. Thank you, Lord, that you are
sufficient and graciously meet my needs.
Isaiah 40:28; John 5:26

I worship You, Lord for You are the God who made
the world and all things in it. Because You are Lord
of the heavens and earth, You do not dwell in temples
made with men's hands; neither are You served by
human hands as though You needed anything, since
You Yourself give to all life and breath and all
things. Blessed be Your name in all the earth.
Acts 17: 24-25

Shepherd – *Jesus as our Shepherd guides us,
protects us, provides for us, and keeps watch over us.*

You are my Shepherd; I shall not be in want for You
make me lie down in green pastures, You lead me
beside still waters. You restore my soul. You guide
me in paths of righteousness for Your own name's
sake. Even though I walk through the valley of the
shadow of death, You are with me, and I will fear no
evil. Your rod and Your staff comfort me. You are
the Good Shepherd, the Great Shepherd. You know
me by name, and I know You, and I am confident
that You will lead me home. You laid down Your life
for Your sheep, therefore I will dwell in Your
presence forever. I will bless Your name for all
eternity.   **Psalm 23; John 10:11-14**

Come, O people, let us worship and bow down; let us kneel before the Lord, our Maker. For he is God, and we are the sheep of His pasture, and the people of His hand. Today, if you hear His voice, do not harden your hearts, but come, for His sheep know His voice and follow Him. **Psalm 95:6-8**

Like a shepherd, You tend Your flock, O Lord. I see Your tenderness as You gather the lambs and carry them in Your arms. I see Your gentleness as you lead the nursing ewes. I worship You for You have tended me. You have gathered me and carried me in Your next to Your heart. You have led me in gentleness, like the only true and great Shepherd that You are.
Isaiah 40:11

You are a God of peace - the great Shepherd of the sheep through the blood of the eternal covenant - Jesus Christ our Lord. **Hebrews 13:20**

Lord Jesus, You are the Great Shepherd, the Chief Shepherd, and I worship You for when You appear, You will give the unfading crown of glory to those who are faithful through the power of Your Holy Spirit. **1 Peter 5:4**

Sovereign – *God is the supreme and preeminent ruler over all His creation. He is Ruler with absolute power and authority. He is above all and is superior to all created things. He alone orchestrates the events of history according to His purpose.*

O my soul, tremble before the great and Sovereign God of all the earth. Let the heavens be glad, and let the earth rejoice. Let them say among the nations, "The Lord reigns!" All the ends of the earth will remember and turn to the Lord, and all the families of the nations will worship before Him, the Most High God. For the kingdom is His and He rules over the nations. Great are You, Sovereign God and greatly to be praised!   **1 Chronicles 16:30-31; Psalm 22:7-8**

You are God, and there is no one like You, for You declare the end from the beginning and from ancient times things which have not been done. You say, "My purpose will be established, and I will accomplish all My good pleasure. Truly I have spoken; truly I will bring it to pass. I have planned it, surely, I will do it." I bow before You for You alone are Sovereign God of the heavens and the earth.
Isaiah 46:8-11

Lord of the heavens and the earth, You have established Your throne in the heavens and Your kingdom rules overall. You are Most High God and worthy to be praised and honored for You live and reign forever and Your dominion is an everlasting dominion, and Your kingdom endures through all generations. You do according to Your perfect will

97

among the host of heaven and among all the inhabitants of the earth. Who could ask You, "What have You done?" for You are sovereign in Your righteousness and in Your good and perfect will. I humbly bow before You.
Psalm 103:19; Daniel 4:34-35

Spirit - *The Holy spirit is a witness of God and Jesus Christ confirming the truth of the gospel. He communicates truth and discernment with saved humanity in a still voice of perfect mildness. He is the third person of the trinity – Father, Son, and Holy Spirit.*

Jesus spoke to the disciples saying, "All authority has been given to Me in heaven and on earth. Go therefore, and make disciples of all the nations, baptizing them in the name of the Father and of the Son and of the Holy Spirit.   **Matthew 28:18-19**

But the fruit of the Spirit is love, joy, peace, patience, kindness, goodness, faithfulness, gentleness, and self-control. Against such there is no law.
Galatians 5:22

The manifestation of the Spirit is given to each one for the profit of all: wisdom, knowledge, faith, gift of healings, worker of miracles, prophecy, and discernment. The same Spirit works all these things, distributing to each one individually as He wills.
1 Corinthians 123:7-11

Supreme – *God is highest in rank, power, and authority. He is superior, to the highest degree, and utmost of all created things. He has the absolute right to do all things according to His own good pleasure.*

By Your word Lord, the heavens were made and by the breath of Your mouth all the hosts of heaven. You gather the waters of the sea together. The earth is full of Your loving kindness. O let the earth fear the Lord and all the inhabitants of the world stand in awe of You. For You spoke and it was done; You commanded, and it stood fast. You nullify the counsel of the nations and frustrate the plans of the peoples. Your counsel stands forever. You are supreme, and blessed is the nation whose God is the Lord.   **Psalm 33:6-11**

We eagerly wait for the day when You, Lord, will be King over all the earth. In that day You will be the only One, the King of kings and the Lord of lords who lives and reigns forever and ever. Your name is the Most High. And we cry out, "Come quickly Lord Jesus!"   **Zechariah 14:9**

Discover God as Savior and Giver of life; marvel at God who is self-existent and self-sufficient who lives and reigns through all eternity; be like a lamb and follow Him as He leads you to nourishment and peace; bow before the Sovereign God of the universe in humble adoration; listen for the still voice of the Holy Spirit to guide you in all your ways, and worship Him as the Supreme God for there is no other.

*****

T

Discover God as

Timeless – *God is not bound by time - He owns time. There is never a time that God was did not exist.*

O Lord, as Moses spoke these words long ago, I join with him, "Lord, You have been our dwelling place in all generations. Before the mountains were born, or You did give birth to the earth and the world, even from everlasting to everlasting, You are God." And the psalmist declares, "Your throne is established from of old; You are from everlasting." And again, the psalmist says, "Of old You did create the earth, and the heavens are the work of Your hands. Even they will perish, but You do endure. You are the same, and your years will not come to an end." You are without beginning and without end and I worship You.   **Psalm 90:1-2, 93:2, 102:25-27**

Heavenly Father, I give thanks to You since every good and perfect gift is from You. You reign down every good gift for You are the Father of lights with whom there is no variation or shadow due to change, and of Your years, there is no end. Blessed be Your name, O Most High and timeless God.
James 1:17

Listen to the words of the Lord God, O peoples of the whole earth, "I am the Alpha and the Omega, who is and who was and who is to come, the Almighty." One day, I know You will be coming with the clouds, and every eye will see You in all Your majesty. Glory and dominion be to You forever and ever, Lord God Almighty. **Revelation 1:6-8**

Transcendent – *God is above and independent of His creation, and He would exist apart from His creation. God is outside of humanity's full perception or grasp.*

Awesome God, Your thoughts are not my thoughts, and my ways are not Your ways. As the heavens are higher than the earth so are Your ways higher than my ways, and Your thoughts higher than my thoughts. Truly, You are above Your creation, O Most High God. **Isaiah 55:8-9**

O the depth of the riches and wisdom and knowledge of God! How unsearchable are Your judgments and how inscrutable are Your ways! For who has known

Your mind, O Lord, or who has been Your counselor or who has given You a gift that he might be re-paid? For from You and through You and to You are all things. To You be praised and glory forever! **Romans 11:33-36**

Trustworthy - *God is true, and anything He says is trustworthy to believe.*

God is not man, that He should lie, nor a son of man, that He should change His mind. Has He said, and will He not do it? Or, has He spoken, and will he not make it good? **Numbers 23:19**

Trust in the Lord forever, for in YAH, the Lord, is everlasting strength. **Isaiah 26:4**

Trust in the Lord with all your strength and lean not on your own understanding; in all your ways acknowledge Him, trust in Him, and He will direct your paths. **Proverbs 3:5-6**

This is a trustworthy saying and deserving of all acceptance, that Christ Jesus came into the world to save sinners. **1 Timothy 1:15**

Truthful – *All that God says is reality. God always speaks with absolute truth in agreement and consistency with all that is represented by God Himself.*

All that God says is reality whether believed by man or not. Hear what the Lord Jesus says to His disciples and to us, "I am the way, and the truth, and the life; no one comes to the Father but through Me." Lord Jesus, You are truth. Your word is truth. We are sanctified in Your truth. I worship You for You are the only begotten from the Father full of grace and truth.   **John 14:3, 6, 17:17**

We know that the Son of God has come and has given us an understanding that we may know Him who is true; and we are in Him who is true, in His Son Jesus Christ. This is the true God and eternal life. **1 John 5:20**

Discover God in His timelessness that is beyond our comprehension and yet, is a reality; worship Him though He is above man's understanding, breathe deeply that we have a God who is completely trustworthy, and learn from Him how to be truthful in all things.

*****

104

U

Discover God as

Unchanging – God never changes in any of His attributes, His holiness, His purposes, and His plans.

You, Lord, in the beginning laid the foundation of the earth. And the heavens are the work of Your hands. They will perish, but You remain; and they will all grow old like a garment; like a cloak You will fold them up, and they will be changed. But you are the same, and Your years will not fail. **Hebrews 1:10-12**

Lord Jesus Christ, I praise You for You are unchangeable. You are the same yesterday and today, yes, and forever. What is man, O Lord? He is like a flower that flourishes in the field and the wind passes over it, and it is no more. But Your loving kindness is from everlasting to everlasting on those who fear You and Your righteousness to children's children for all generations. Great is the Lord and greatly to be praised for Your mercy endures forever.
Psalm 103:15-18; Hebrews 13:8

The grass withers, the flower fades, but the word of our God will stand forever. What joy fills my soul!
Isaiah 40:8

Every good gift and every perfect gift are from You, coming down from You, Father of lights with whom there is no variation or shadow due to change.
James 1:17

Unique – *There is none like Him; He is the one and only Creator, Lord, King, and triune God – Father, Son, and Holy Spirit, and is from everlasting to everlasting.*

Who is like You among the gods, O Lord? Who compares to You, majestic in holiness and awesome in praises, working marvelous wonders? You show Your greatness and Your strong hand for what god is there in heaven or on earth who could do such works and mighty acts as You? I take to heart that You, Lord, are God in heaven and on earth—there is no other god like you, for all the gods of the peoples are worthless idols.
Exodus 15:11; Deuteronomy 3:24, 39

There is no one like You, God of the heavens and the earth. All the gods of the peoples are worthless idols, but You are the only true God. There are no works like Your works, for You are great and You do wondrous deeds. You alone are God. I praise You and worship You. You have said, "Know and believe Me, and understand that I am He. Before Me there

was no god formed, and there is no Savior besides Me." "It is I who have declared and saved and proclaimed. You are my witnesses, I am God." As Lord of Hosts, You have also said, "I am the first and the last, and there is no god besides Me. Again, You have said, "Is there any God besides Me, or is there any other rock? I know of none." Therefore, I acknowledge and believe You are the true God and there is no other.
Psalm 86:8-10; Isaiah 43:10-12, 44:6-8

Unsearchable – *God's perfect wisdom that cannot be searched is inscrutable; hidden, and man can never discover all that God is.*

You are exalted. The number of Your years is unsearchable. We do not know the activity of You, God, who makes all things. Your greatness is unsearchable to any human mind.
Job 36:26; Ecclesiastes 11:5

Oh, the depth of Your riches both of wisdom and knowledge, O God of the highest heaven! How unsearchable are Your judgments and unfathomable are Your ways! Who has known the mind of the Lord or who has been a counselor to You? Or who has given You a gift that he should be paid back? Lord, from You and through You and to You are all things. To You be glory forever! **Romans 11:33-36**

Discover God and be amazed that He never changes, He never sleeps, or needs to eat; He is unique in every way and there in no god like Him. Anticipate eternity because it will take all of eternity for Him to reveal all His unsearchable, hidden mysteries to His redeemed people.

*****

$\mathcal{V}$

Discover God as

Victorious – *God is triumphant in all that he does. No one and nothing can triumph over God.*

In God we boast all day long and praise Your name forever. You have accomplished victory on our behalf. You are our King, O God; command victories for Your people. **Psalm 44:4, 8**

Lord, You swallowed up death for all time. How I worship You for You trampled over death with death and rose victorious. We need not fear, but we can be assured, and we can say, "O death, where is your victory? O death where is your sting?" Thanks be to You, Lord God, who gives us the victory through our Lord and Savior Jesus Christ. You have overcome the world, and we too can be overcomers through faith in You, our mighty King and victorious Lord.
Isaiah 25:8; 1 Corinthians 15:54-55; 1 John 5:4

Who but You, Lord, could wipe away all our tears? Who but You could abolish death forevermore? Who but You, could do away with sin and the penalty of sin, sorrow, sickness, pain and crying, death and mourning? Who but You could comfort us with the comfort of One who has overcome? I humble myself before You, Jesus. I bow before You in awe for you are my Victor and my Salvation.   **Revelation 21:4**

Discover God as the victorious God who triumphs in all He does, who abolished death, who overcame the world, and who paid the penalty for all sin for all time.

*****

W

Discover God as

Wise - _God's wisdom goes beyond knowledge and understanding and leads Him to always make right choices. God is the source of all wisdom and knowledge._

God of the heavens and all creation, I join my heart in agreement with Daniel of old when he said, "Blessed be the name of God forever and ever to whom belong wisdom and might for You change the times and the seasons; You remove kings and set up kings; You give wisdom to wise men and knowledge to men of understanding. Apart from You, there is nothing known that is known for it is You who reveals the profound and hidden things. You know what is in the darkness for darkness is as light to You. You are the Light, and we have our understanding in You, O blessed Lord God. **Daniel 2:20-22**

Lord Jesus, how good it is to know that when You left Your throne of glory and came to earth, born of a woman, putting on flesh and blood, that as a child, You grew and became strong and were filled with wisdom. The favor of Your Father in heaven was upon You, and all who heard You speak marveled at

111

Your words. I too stand in awe of who You are. I give praise and adoration to You for You are the source of all wisdom. **Luke 2:40**

To God our Savior, who alone is wise, be glory and majesty, dominion, and power, both now and forever. **Jude 25**

Wonderful - *Wise teaching comes from the Lord of hosts, who is wonderful in counsel and excellent in guidance, and marvelous in works.*

Many, O Lord my God, are Your wonderful works which You have done; and Your thoughts toward us cannot be recounted to You in order; if I would declare and speak of them, they are more than can be numbered. **Psalm 40:5**

For unto *us* a Child is born, unto us a Son is given; and the government will be upon His shoulder. And His name will be called Wonderful, Counselor, Mighty God, Everlasting Father, Prince of Peace. **Isiah 9:6**

Worthy - *God has excellence, merit, and virtue. He alone is deserving of honor, worship, and praise.*

A strong angel proclaimed in a loud voice, "Who is worthy to open the book and to break its seals?" And no one in heaven or on earth or under the earth was able to open the book or to look into it. Then one of the elders in heaven said, "The Lion that is from the tribe of Judah, the Root of David, has overcome so as to open the book and its seven seals." It is then that I realized that You, Lord Jesus, are competent and worthy to break the seven seals and open the scroll to release the plagues for the power to open the seals does not come in strength, but in worth. And You alone, O Lord, are worthy to be worshipped. Lord Jesus, how we rejoice to know that the four living creatures and the elders of heaven fall before You, O Lamb of God who was slain. We bow in awe as they sing a new song, "Worthy are You to take the book and break its seals for You were slain and did purchase for God with Your blood men from every tribe and tongue and peoples and nations." Blessings and honor and glory be to You, O worthy One. **Revelation 5:2-5, 9**

Wrathful – *There is within God a hatred for all that is unrighteous and a desire to punish all unrighteousness. Whatever is inconsistent with His holy standard must be atoned for or consumed. God is provoked to fierce anger because of sin. Without an understanding of God's just response to sin, Jesus' cross and the gospel do not make sense.*

I tremble at the way Your people because of their rebellion, their abominations, and their wicked deeds in the wilderness provoked You to wrath - so much so that You would have destroyed them. **Deuteronomy 9:7-8**

We cannot maintain a right view of God without understanding the seriousness of His wrath. "If only we knew the power of Your anger! Your wrath is as great as the fear that is Your due." **Psalm 90:11**

I fear for those outside Your grace for You are a jealous, avenging, and wrathful God. You take vengeance on Your adversaries, and You reserve Your wrath for Your enemies. Your wrath is just and holy against sin and your mercies and grace are abundant toward those who repent. **Nahum 1:2**

Discover God as the only wise God and wonderful Counselor. Humble yourself before the Lamb, Jesus Christ, the only One found worthy to open the seals of the scroll releasing the judgments of God's wrath against sin and those who refused God's offer of salvation by rejecting the Christ.

$\mathcal{X}$

Discover God as

eXalted - *God is high, elevated, glorified and extolled above everything and everyone.*

Be still, O people, and know that God is God. He will be exalted among the nations; He will be exalted in the earth. Man will be humbled, and the Lord alone will be exalted. **Psalm 46:10; Isaiah 2:11**

Lord Jesus, You are the One whom God exalted to His right hand as a Prince and a Savior to grant forgiveness of sins through repentance. You alone are worthy to be seated in the place of honor - at the right hand of God. I praise You for You are high and lifted and are the exalted One of God. **Acts 5:31**

Christ Jesus, it is good for us to know that although You existed in the form of God - of the same nature and essence of God, You did not think this something to be exploited to Your own advantage. I marvel that You would enter this dark world, coming as the Light to all men, in order to die a shameful death on the cross for our sake. No wonder God highly exalted You and gave the name that is above every name that at the name of Jesus, every knee in heaven and on

115

earth and under the earth will bow, and every tongue will confess that You are Lord to the glory of Your Father. O, how I magnify Your name and lift it high. **Philippians 2:9**

eXtraordinary – No one or nothing could attain to God's exceptional likeness.

O Lord, our Lord, how excellent is Your name in all the earth, who have set Your glory above the heavens!   **Psalm 8:1**

"For My thoughts are not your thoughts, nor are your ways My ways," says the Lord. "For as the heavens are higher than the earth, so are My ways higher than your ways, and My thoughts than your thoughts. **Isaiah 55:8-9**

Now God worked unusual miracles by the hands of Paul, so that even handkerchiefs or aprons were brought from his body to the sick, and the diseases left them, and the evil spirits went out of them. **Acts 19:11**

Xristos **(Greek for Christ) -** *The title and name, given to Jesus second person of the trinity – Father, Son, and Holy Spirit.*

The gospel of Matthew lists the genealogy of Jesus Christ from Abraham to Joseph, the earthly father of Jesus. Matthew concludes the genealogy of Jesus saying, "And Jacob begot Joseph the husband of Mary, of whom was born Jesus who is called Christ." "And Mary will bring forth a Son, and you shall call His name Jesus, for He will save his people from their sins." **Matthew 1:1,16,21**

Discover God as the exalted One ; praise Him because He is extraordinary, and worship Him as Xristos - the Christ.

*****

Y

Discover God as

Yahweh (YHWH) – _Yahweh is God's highest name and is the principal name in the Old Testament by which God revealed Himself. It is the most sacred, distinctive, and incommunicable name of God. God's name means LORD, Jehovah. It was considered irreverent to utter the name of Yahweh, so it was only written and never spoken. Jehovah is a variation of Yahweh and occurs 6,823 times in the Old Testament and is especially associated with God's holiness. In the Hebrew Bible, it means the great I AM. I AM WHO I AM._

"I AM WHO I AM." You are the One who is Yahweh! You are the active, self-existent One and Israel's Redeemer. You are holy and You hate sin, and yet, Your gracious provision of redemption extends to even me; and not to me only, but to all who believe in the name of Your Son, Jesus, my Lord, and my God. **Exodus 3:14**

Your name alone is Jehovah for You are the Most High over all the earth. You, God, are my salvation; I will trust and not be afraid for You, Jehovah God are my strength and my song, and You have become my salvation. **Psalm 83:18; Isaiah 12:2**

Discover God as Yahweh and bow in humble exaltation of a most holy God!

*****

Z

Discover God as

Zealous - *God is passionate and fervently pursues His purposes.*

Of the increase of His government and peace there will be no end. Upon the throne of David and over His kingdom, to order it and establish it with judgment and justice from that time forward, even forever. The zeal of the Lord of Hosts will perform this. **Isaiah 9:7**

O Lord, You will be zealous for Your land, and You will have pity on Your people. You gave Yourself for our sake to redeem us from every lawless deed and to purify for Yourself a people for Your own possession. You are a God zealous for good deeds. **Joel 2:18; Titus 2:14**

Listen to what the Lord of hosts says, "I am zealous for Jerusalem with great zeal; with great fervor I am zealous for her." O how You long to bless Your people with Your presence and yearn for them to worship You. I worship You, for You are zealous for our good. **Zechariah 8:2**

Discover God as the King eternal, immortal, invisible, and give glory to God who alone is wise be honor and glory forever and ever.

Psalms 18:30-31 – As for God, His way is blameless; the word of the Lord is flawless. He is a shield to all who take refuge in Him.

Meet the Author

Rita Kroon was born in Minneapolis, but raised in St. Paul, MN. She graduated from Sibley High School and received her AA degree in speech/ communications from Lakewood Community College.

She is an author, blogger, and Bible study group leader. She has written women's Bible studies, devotionals, novels (contemporary and historical), wildlife magazine articles, children's short stories, poetry, a humorous newspaper column "Rita Raps it up," and more.

Her current works are in memory of her husband, Burt, and their daughter, René. She has two other daughters, LaDawn and Shelly, and 17 grandchildren. She resides in Lexington, MN.

OTHER BOOKS BY RITA KROON

Cancer – a Journey through the Valley is a personal memoir. Rita Kroon shares her journey through the valley where she realized that her faith in God during the calm seasons of life necessitated a mighty strengthening if it were to sustain her on the battlefield. Discover how God worked such a faith while she was in the throes of cancer. Be amazed at the sovereignty of God to heal some; stand in awe to see His grace given to those for whom He has a different purpose. Know that the God who guides our steps is the same God who directs our stops. This is a story of hope and trust in the valley.

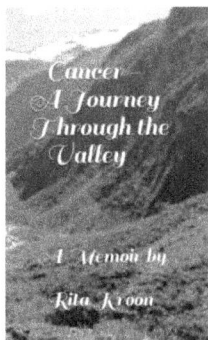

ISBN: 9780989198516

Praying the Scriptures is a collection of prayers and promises taken from God's Word, since no word of God shall be void of power. When words cannot be found to say what is on your heart, this collection of prayers is meant to guide you during those times of solitude. If praying is unfamiliar to you, or perhaps has long ago been abandoned, this book provides one way to begin afresh. There is no prayer like that which forms itself in the words and thoughts of Scripture, for there are no other words on earth spoken by man that have neither more power nor more truth than God's Word.

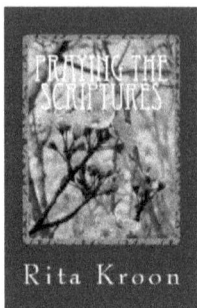

ISBN: 9780989198585

Kiss Your Mommy Goodbye is a contemporary novel. In his desperate quest to provide love and stability as a part-time father to young Maddy, Mike does the unthinkable. His actions got far more disastrous results than he could have ever imagined, and the very one he tried to protect would suffer the repercussions of his decision. In this riveting tale, a man struggles to reconcile and rebuild broken relationships and find peace with others and with God. **ISBN: 9780989198561**

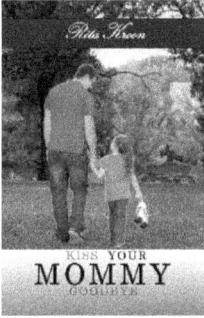

Womanhood: Becoming a Woman of Virtue

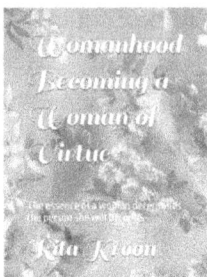

is an eight-week, interactive Bible study of eight inspirational women of the Old Testament and is suitable for individual or group setting. There are two sections: in-depth for the woman who likes to linger in the Word or condensed for the woman on the go. Explore the lives of Eve, Sarah, Rebekah, Rachel, Miriam, Deborah, Tamar, and Esther–ordinary women who find themselves in unprecedented circumstances. Be inspired by their faith, encouraged through their hardships, and challenged by their choices and decisions as you seek to become a woman of virtue. **ISBN: 9780989198554**

Letters from the Past is historical fiction. Seven women of the Bible write personal letters to today's woman. Each woman reveals the emotional impact that infertility, rape, incest, deception and betrayal, and family dysfunction had on her. In each of their stories, trial turns to triumph when the thread of God's faithfulness is traced through these women of ancient times to the women of the twenty first century. Today's woman will be challenged and encouraged, find hope for the oppressed, and celebrate the accomplishments of Sarah, Rebekah, Rachel, Miriam, Deborah, Tamar, and Esther.

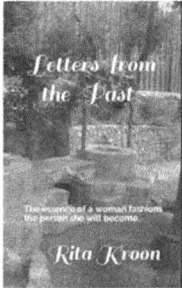

ISBN: 9780989198578

40 Days of Assurance is a daily devotional intended to give you assurance in your walk with God, or with your parenting skills, or with relationships, or with a lack of confidence with who you are as a person. Sometimes we just need loving arms around us; to be assured that everything will work out. Bring your empty cup to the Lord that He may fill it with your daily portion of His grace and discover the peace of God that surpasses all understanding that will keep your heart and mind in Christ Jesus. ISBN:9780989198530

40 Days of Encouragement is a daily devotional when you may feel like giving up, or you are bombarded with negative thoughts, or you have lost all hope, or you are despairing over broken relationships, or when you see the future through the bleakness of the past. Look up! Be uplifted. God is a reservoir of strength. Come. Drink deeply of God's word and be encouraged. **ISBN**: **9780989198547**

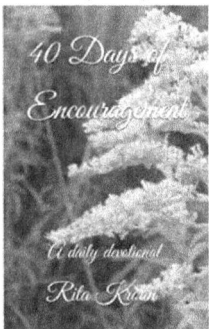

40 Days in the Wilderness is a daily devotional that gives insight to strengthen and to nourish you as you journey through your wilderness – a drought in your spiritual walk? A desert in your marriage with no oasis in sight? A dry spell at work or at school? Lacking peace amidst the chaos? Take heart. Bring your empty cup to the Lord that He may fill with your daily portion of His grace and mercy new every morning. Find the faith needed to sustain you. Be nourished and refreshed. **ISBN: 9780989198509**

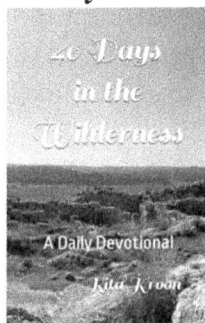

Nuggets From My *Pocket* is a collection of tidbits of wisdom quotes, sayings, blessings, promises and more that have been gathered along the trail. These gems of truth will inspire and encourage you. They will give you cause to pause, time to wonder and ponder, and a reason to reflect.

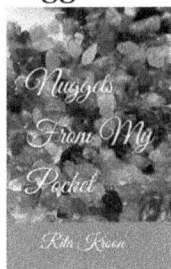

Nuggets From My Pocket is my gift to you for your pocket, or to share a nugget of encouragement with those around you

Here's a nugget to ponder: "God gives evidence of His existence, but not proof since He always leaves room for faith." **ISBN: 9780989198592**

__More Nuggets From My Pocket__ is a collection of sayings, wit, insights, quotes, wisdom, promises, prayer, and more that were gathered where the trail led to an open meadow.

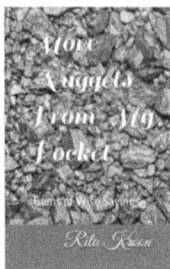

These gems will inspire you and encourage you no matter what path of life you travel. Stop to ponder the insights given, or to discover a fresh perspective, or to glean new meaning to old sayings.

__More Nuggets From My Pocket__ is my way of giving you such an opportunity to explore rather than to merely hurry on your way. You may even want to share a nugget with a friend to encourage.

ISBN: 9798682187225

Extra Nuggets From My Pocket is a collection of sayings meant to stir your imagination, fill your heart, and satisfy your desire for fresh "Ah, moments."

When the path of life leads me beside still waters, I search the beach for Extra Nuggets like one does when looking for agates on the North Shore. Some of these gems of truth, wit, quotes, prayers, blessings, and more are mine and some are those I gathered along the way and tucked into my pocket.

Come, walk with me along the beach and discover *Extra Nuggets* for your pocket or to share with a friend along the way.

ISBN: 9798587330566

133

Almost-Forgotten Nuggets is a collection of truthful, inspiring, and wise sayings, and follows the footprints of its three siblings, ***Nuggets From My Pocket, More Nuggets From My Pocket,*** **and** ***Extra Nuggets From My Pocket***. The path is familiar, but the landscape has an added dimension of newness that makes a pleasant journey most memorable.

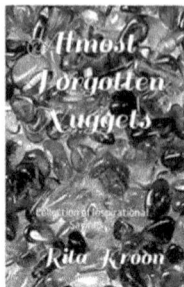

Almost-Forgotten Nuggets is sure to take you on an adventure much like a treasure hunt where one seeks the next gem to keep for your pocket or to share with a friend along the way.

Here is a preview of what is inside - "Unconfessed sin is like a math problem: it divides the heart; adds woes; subtracts peace, and it multiplies consequences."

Another peek – "It is sometimes difficult, but always good, to trust God with who you treasure most in this world."

ISBN: 9798511772042

John ~ A Mini Study is an interactive Bible study of the Gospel of John and is suitable for individual and group setting. It uses a loosely structured <u>Observation</u>, <u>Interpretation,</u> and <u>Application</u> method of study with summarizing <u>Principles</u> in an easy-to-read format. One way to think of it like this: The *observation of facts* is like reading a menu. The *interpretation* is looking at the number of calories or the price on the menu. The *application questions* are the main course – the most satisfying part of the meal that energizes us for action. The *principle* is the appetizer that sharpens our desire for what is coming next. *Something to ponder* is the dessert and like most desserts, is just an occasional treat.

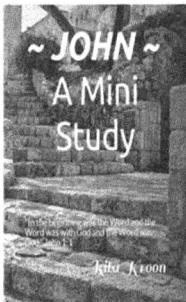

We learn what we can, apply what we know, and leave the rest to **God** is the *gratuity* we leave for the one who gave us dinner out ~ John, the disciple whom Jesus loved. If we set a goal to connect with God and His truth every time we study His Word, we allow Him to mature us in our walk of faith.

"This is the disciple who testifies of these things and wrote these things, and we know this testimony is true." John 21:24 "BEHOLD! The Lamb of God!"
ISBN: 9798545633234

Pebbles of Truth is a collection of short, timeless sayings of truth that are filled with wisdom, give great insight, plus unforgettable quotes, encouragement, blessings, thoughts to remember, and explore God's greatness. These pebbles of truth connect the heart with one's imagination much like pebbles on a beach connect the water and the land.

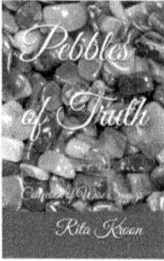

Here is a sneak peek: "Learn to write your hurts in the sand and to carve your blessings in stone." Here's another: "Man contributed nothing to his salvation except the sin that made it necessary."

Pebbles of Truth is sure to give you a delightful reading and sharing experience.

ISBN: 9798842917037

Come, join me for A Walk to the Well ~
A Place for Women to find Encouragement,
Hope, and Inspiration.

www.awalktothewell.com

www.ingramcontent.com/pod-product-compliance
Lightning Source LLC
Chambersburg PA
CBHW060255050426
42448CB00009B/1652